— REMEMBERING —

Kingstree

South Carolina

—— REMEMBERING ——

Kingstree
South Carolina

THE COLLECTED WRITINGS OF
BESSIE SWANN BRITTON

Edited by LINDA W. BROWN

Charleston London

History
PRESS

Published by The History Press
Charleston, SC 29403
www.historypress.net

Front cover: This view, looking north on Academy Street, shows the white picket fences that enclosed yards early in the last century. *Photograph courtesy of Williamsburgh Historical Museum.*

First published 2007

Manufactured in the United Kingdom

ISBN 978.1.59629.291.8

Library of Congress CIP data applied for.

Dedicated to the memory of my mother, Katherine B. Brown, who taught me to love a good story, and to my father, John S. Brown Jr., who continues to make me believe I can accomplish whatever I put my mind to.

Contents

Contents

Acknowledgements

No book comes into being in a vacuum. I am especially grateful to Joanne Brown, director of the Williamsburgh Historical Museum, for her help and support in this endeavor. She, Ann McConnell and Edward Eatmon took time to go through rolls of microfilm in search of these columns that were printed long ago. Joanne and Bruce Brown also spent time looking through the museum's extensive collection to find pictures that match the stories in this book. In addition, Joanne read the manuscript while taking care of her other duties. My thanks to all of them.

I would like to thank Barry Schweickert for his eagle-eyed proofreading and for giving me free reign in his home office for the past year as I've transcribed, edited and prepared these stories for publication. I'm sure my clutter has offended the neatness of his soul, but he has not expressed those feelings out loud.

Lee Gordon Brockington and Bubber Jenkinson, both of whom have had books published in the last year, have been sources of encouragement. I would especially like to thank Lee for mentioning my name to Kirsty Sutton and Jenny Kaemmerlen at The History Press.

Introduction

Bessie Swann was born August 13, 1894. Very early in her life, her father moved the family to a farm just outside Kingstree, South Carolina. They lived there until his unexpected death in 1900. Then, his widow left the farm and moved her three small daughters to Kingstree. Bessie grew up in Kingstree and later married her high school sweetheart, John Britton.

During the 1950s, she felt the need to put many of her memories of growing up in the village on paper. The local newspaper then, the *County Record*, published those musings under the title, "Then and Now, or Tales of Long Ago." The column had a large following, evidenced by the number of letters she received each week. After a time, however, the columns ceased to be published.

In the 1970s, Dr. Charles Preacher pleaded with *County Record* publisher Myrtle Cromer to reprint the old Bessie Britton columns. Mrs. Cromer agreed, and "Miss Bessie," as she was known far and wide, began rewriting those stories—and adding a few more for good measure.

I was in high school when the columns were reprinted, and while I had forgotten many of the details, I remembered the pleasure I got from reading them. Last year, while compiling a column of tidbits from old newspapers for Kingstree's current weekly, the *News*, I once again ran across the Bessie Britton columns. I began transcribing them, and as I worked, I had the idea to compile them into a book. That way, those who had enjoyed them in the past, those new to Kingstree and those from other towns and cities throughout the country who have an interest in the past and in small towns would get a chance to read about some of the remarkable people and events that have made this town what it is today.

Several times in the postscripts that accompanied many of Bessie Britton's columns, letter writers encouraged her to publish a book. She always demurred, citing the cost of publishing a book that she felt would appeal only to a limited audience. She also modestly claimed that she was merely a "scribbler," not a writer, and that her only desire was to preserve some of the stories that make up the history of the area. In one instance, however, she did note that she hoped that at some later time her work would be looked at for its historical value. That time is now, and I am profoundly grateful to be the instrument through which these tales live, for Bessie Swann Britton was far more than a mere scribbler; she was the consummate storyteller.

I have tried to blend the two versions of the stories (those from the '50s and those from the '70s) into a coherent whole while keeping the best of both. Please remember as you read that many of the landmarks have changed—in some cases, more than once. As an example, the lot on which the Kingstree Academy sat during Bessie Swann's school days later became the home of the Carnegie Library, which now houses the Williamsburgh Historical Museum.

Bessie Britton was a plainspoken woman who wrote long before the world ever heard of the concept of political correctness. Some of her assertions may sound rather harsh to our politically correct sensitivities, but I ask that you remember the times in which these columns were written and take her comments accordingly.

We owe much to Miss Bessie for writing these tales of long ago and to Mrs. Cromer for printing them. Without them, we would no longer remember much of the rich history of this community during the early twentieth century.

Linda W. Brown
Kingstree, South Carolina

Part I
Village Life

Marshmallows

Another new year for Kingstree makes me realize with a sickening thud that I can remember fifty previous new years for Kingstree, which is the seat of Williamsburg County in South Carolina. At the turn of the century, Kingstree was surrounded by farms on which cotton was king and there was no competition from synthetics. The growing of tobacco and truck crops had not yet been introduced, and nobody had ever heard of a boll weevil.

The two longest streets were Main and Academy and the chief business district spread around their intersection. Both ends of those two streets extended into choice residential areas. About half the men living in town commuted to their farms on horseback or in buggies, as automobiles were unknown. There were no paved roads and no highway department. Also, there were no radios, no record players, no TVs and no movies.

For musical entertainment, we had only pianos, harps, organs, horns and stringed instruments. Most little girls and a few little boys took piano lessons and hated them and the suffering victims who taught them. But we never tired of practicing on mouth organs and Jew's harps, which we thought were named juice harps because we blew so much spit learning to play them. The older boys could make music of sorts blowing on combs with tissue paper pressed against them or by banging silver spoons against their knees.

The two wooden stores I remember best were on each side of the courthouse square on Main Street. Mr. George S. Barr ran a grocery store where the *County Record* is now. The newspaper was then published by a good-looking man named Bristow in a cottage on the southwest corner of Main and Jackson Streets, where the Hammet house now stands. Bristow was courting Miss Barbara Jacobs, but she married W.I. Nexsen. However, Bristow must have found another love, as he now has a daughter—the popular author Gwen Bristow.

One day Mother sent my sister Mary and me to Barr's grocery with five cents for two pairs of shoestrings and a penny each for candy. I was a lively little tomboy with my sandy hair bobbed like Buster Brown in the funny papers. I was always getting into scrapes, but Mary, who was three years older, never got into scrapes. She was a beautiful child with soulful brown eyes, long brown curls and rosy cheeks, and I thought she looked like Jesus, except that her dark curls hung farther down her back.

She and I were the only customers in the grocery, so we took our time drooling over the penny candies in the glass showcase. Mr. Barr, a jolly man, was opening a peck-sized wooden box, carefully extracting each small nail with a claw hammer and tossing it into a nearby keg, possibly to be sold.

Every store had printed mottos hanging in full view. They said, "Waste not, want not," or "A penny saved is a penny made," or "Take care of the pennies, and the dollars will take care of themselves." No doubt such slogans influenced the thinking of a whole generation who read them for years. Mother still quotes a favorite to her grandchildren: "Use your head more and your feet less, and you will arrive sooner."

I, too, was influenced by them. For instance, I have wished many times that somebody would write about the ordinary doings in our village long ago, lest such information be lost forever when my generation dies. But nobody did. One day, when I wondered if I could do it myself, an old slogan popped into my mind: "What you can do—or think you can—begin it."

In the showcase there were lemon and peppermint sticks, colored gumdrops and bilious green suckers. There were also chocolate drops with white centers, chocolate cigars and chocolate soldiers in Confederate uniforms. There were striped jawbreakers, flavored with horehound. They were too big to get into a child's mouth, and Mother wouldn't let us chop them with the hatchet. I thought she meant that we might damage the hatchet. There were tiny, fluted pie plates of tin, each with its tin spoon bogged down in a red mixture, and black iron frying pans the size of a silver dollar, each containing a candy fried egg, sunny-side-up. Also, there were long, round sticks of so-called chewing gum—twice the size of a pencil and snow white—but they were really sweetened beeswax. Each item sold for one cent.

Children were seldom given more than a penny to spend at a time. The South, which had lost the War Between the States, was still struggling. Southerners were the only people in the United States ever to know what it was to have their own homes overrun by half-drunken soldiers of a conquering army enjoying their vengeance. Confederate money was no longer any good except to paste on decorative screens. New money was scarce in the South and was carefully hoarded, as everyone was still

Main Street in Kingstree as it looked in the early part of the twentieth century. *Photograph courtesy of Williamsburgh Historical Museum.*

uncertain about the future. There were no such things as welfare or social security, but people helped each other. We impish youngsters were so wonderfully happy with our families and playmates, we didn't even know the South needed help.

However, Southerners still had three things going for them—pride, love of home and sense of humor. "I'm poor but proud" became a popular jest still heard every now and then. I don't know who coined the phrase, "The South will rise again," but in the old days when some discouraged soul quoted it, trying to boost his own spirits, a friend was sure to ask with a deadpan expression, "When?"

White and Colored children played together in the yards and streets every spare moment, fighting and making up when the occasion arose. We neither knew nor cared anything about the political Civil War, its reasons or its results. All joyfully sang, "Dixie" together, for sunny Dixie meant home to all. Nobody paid any attention to race one way or the other. We accepted white and black skin as naturally as we accepted daylight and dark. Both had been with us every day of our lives.

Mary and I finally decided to buy one of the iron frying pans and a stick of gum. As she said, we could eat the candy eggs and then use the pan in our playhouse. When neighborhood boys (we had no brothers) robbed another bird nest and gave us a cracked egg, we could cook it in our pan. And we knew from experience that we could re-sweeten the gum by dipping the wads into Mother's sugar dish when she wasn't looking.

Mr. Barr invited Mary and me to try the new candy in the square box he had just opened. We had never before laid eyes on marshmallows, and I suspected a trick. I thought them dabs of raw biscuit dough dusted with flour, but I was too shy to say so. I kept mine clutched in my fist, and when Mary whispered, "Say 'thank you, sir,'" I wouldn't utter it and merely shut my fist tight on the gummy thing. Mary had never seen a marshmallow, either, but she was born with good manners, so she thanked Mr. Barr prettily and bit into hers, no doubt feeling like the first person to taste a raw oyster, and told Mr. Barr it was good.

I didn't believe her, so once outside the store, I handed her my gummy mass and wiped my hand on my pink chambray dress, saying I couldn't eat dough. Mary ate it with relish. She said the stuff was sweet and let me lick her hand to prove it. One taste of that powdered sugar and I tried to fight her for eating my marshmallow, so she told Mother that I wouldn't thank Mr. Barr and had wiped my hand on my new dress.

Mother chuckled but threatened to spank next time, and she wouldn't let me go back with Mary for the shoestrings we had forgotten. Mr. Barr gave Mary another marshmallow, which she brought home without squashing it. She let me bite the first half, but only after she had marked a dividing line with a pencil. I still like marshmallows.

Material from columns originally published in January 1952 and January 1970.

Dolls from Miss Sally

When I was small, Mr. and Mrs. Bill Lee had a dry goods store on the eastern side of the courthouse square in Kingstree. Mrs. Lee's sister, Miss Sally Wilson, lived with them in the rear of the wooden store.

Miss Sally, a sedate little lady, was regarded as getting along in years, as she was in her mid-twenties and hadn't yet "snagged" a husband. When a customer entered Lee's store—and it isn't likely that happened every day—a bell tinkled mysteriously, and Miss Sally or Miss Jenny appeared just as mysteriously through the dark curtains covering another door. One day, Mother took her three little daughters there. Eula, several years younger than I, was still a babe in swaddling clothes—and I mean *swaddling*. How an infant of that era kept from dying of heat prostration is beyond me.

A baby's clothes were a full yard longer than the baby. The poor little thing had to wear a wide bellyband wrapped snugly around its middle 'til it was eighteen months old. Many were the doleful tales of calamities befalling babies whose bellybands were discarded too soon. In summer, the outline of the flannel was plainly marked on the infant's skin by a rash of red heat bumps. Then there was the long-sleeved undershirt, a white flannel petticoat edged with hand-embroidered scallops, and at least one, but more often two, very elaborately trimmed cotton petticoats. The dress boasted many yards of insertion, lace or frills—or all three—not to mention tiny hand-run tucks. Then an embroidered jacket of wool cashmere called a sack was added, and then a fancy bonnet called a cap, with its ribbon streamers tied into a bow under the baby's chin. A quilted bib, edged with lace, had ribbon streamers tied around the baby's neck with a bow in the back. The bib was to protect the other finery when the baby threw up.

No self-respecting mother neglected to starch her baby's dress and cotton petticoats. The starch was made of strained rice gruel, better for delicate

The Williamsburg County Courthouse as it looked many years ago. *Photograph courtesy of Williamsburgh Historical Museum.*

fabrics than the popular celluloid starch, which made men's collars and cuffs (detached) and shirt fronts (tucked) stiff as the proverbial board.

The baby also wore wool stockings pinned to its diaper and wool booties on its feet. Finally, it was wrapped in a big, fluffy wool shawl with three-inch fringes, blue for boys and pink for girls. But the baby did have two lucky breaks. First, airtight plastic pants had not been invented. Second, mothers were too wise to fall for advertisements for baby oils. They said that oil would clog every pore and make a baby hotter than a pudding. Also, they knew that nothing was so soothing to a rash on babies or fat ladies and gents than a very light dusting of sifted cornstarch (not to be confused with laundry starch), which is still for sale in grocery stores.

I don't remember what Mother bought in Lee's store that day, but Miss Sally thrilled my older sister Mary and me by giving us each a little china doll. They were about the size of a man's finger and had painted faces with blue eyes and long plaits of real hair, very yellow, which was almost as long as the dolls themselves. They sold for a penny apiece.

Mary already had a beautiful French doll about fifteen inches tall with a china head and shoulders and a cloth body, but mine had met a sad fate soon after Santa Claus brought it. When I heard somebody say that the cloth bodies were stuffed with sawdust, I began to wonder what sawdust looked like. Pretty soon I got a hatchet and found out. I didn't think much of sawdust.

I still played with my doll's head with its pretty painted face and white shoulders that must have been made of bone china, and I carefully tied its clothes around its neck to keep it warm. When rocking it to sleep, I would whisper in its ear that I loved it better than anybody in the world except my little baby sister and was sorry I had hurt it. But I wouldn't let Mother or Mary hear me.

Mary's doll was named Juliet, but mine was named Jake, which was a popular name for a mule. I liked animals, and maybe I was friendly with a mule named Jake. I don't remember now.

Material from columns originally published in January 1952 and January 1970.

Brick Stores

The first brick store in Kingstree was Reddick's Red Hot Racket Emporium at 110 W. Main Street. "Red Hot" meant goods priced to sell. "Racket" meant departments and "Emporium" meant dry goods of every kind in stock.

Mr. and Mrs. Henry Reddick later built a rambling frame dwelling on the northeast corner of Ashton Avenue and Gordon Street.

Once when Mr. Reddick was having a half-price sale, Emma Maria Brockington and I decided that was our chance to bedeck our dolls with penny ribbon. We knew that Mr. Reddick couldn't cut a penny in half so he must be giving it away, but when we timidly asked the sale price, he laughed and said it was two yards for one cent. We didn't have a cent, so we sheepishly told him that we would be back later, knowing full well that we wouldn't. When we got our hands on another penny, it would go for one of those new all-day suckers, bright red and so big that one would last the two of us many hours—that is, if we could manage to dodge pesky friends sure to have a hungry-dog look in their eyes when they begged us for a few sucks.

I think J.E. Porter's Grocery was the next brick store to be built in Kingstree. It still stands on the northwest corner of Main and Jackson Streets, and is now occupied by Dr. Paul S. Watson's offices and Claude J. Thompson's Better Homes Service. Mr. Porter had formerly done business in the wooden storeroom still standing next door on Main Street.

Mr. Porter, who never married, was an uncle of Edward and Marie Nelson who now live in the old Porter home surrounded by beautiful flowers and shrubbery facing the post office. He had a reputation for being a scrupulously honest man, and if a customer asked for three

Reddick's Red Hot Racket Emporium is credited with being the first brick store in Kingstree. *Photograph courtesy of Williamsburgh Historical Museum.*

pounds of salt meat and the scales registered a fraction of an ounce underweight, Mr. Porter added a spoonful of salt to make the scales balance. If they showed a little overweight, he scraped off a bit of salt and tossed it back into the wooden meat bin. Hundreds of people in the county wouldn't trade elsewhere the many years Mr. Jim was in business.

One day when I was hardly tall enough to see over the counter, Mother sent me to his grocery. Though I went there often, I was afraid of Mr. Jim, who was a stout man of few words and not given to jesting. When he gruffly asked, "What is it, Bessie?" I uneasily handed him my dime and said, "Two cakes of soap, please, sir."

He asked, "Octagon or Fairy?" Those were the only two brands known, not counting homemade lye soap which was used with long-handled push brushes made of corn shucks to scour kitchen floors 'til they were bleached white. A sprinkling of coarse sand was used on stubborn stains. The lye soap was also used every Monday, as that was washday, and white clothes were boiled in a black iron washpot in every backyard.

My mind had gone blank and I had no idea which soap Mother wanted. Then I suddenly remembered and piped out, "Sweet soap, please, sir." Mr. Porter chuckled and handed me two large, white, oval cakes. The trademark

The Porter House as it looked when occupied by the Nelsons. *Photograph courtesy of Williamsburgh Historical Museum.*

The Porter House still stands, although the porches have been enclosed, and it is now used as a barber/beauty college. *Photograph by Linda Brown.*

on each wrapper was a beautiful little girl with short blonde curls who didn't look a thing like me. She was smiling like an angel and asking, "Have you a little Fairy in your home?" As I skedaddled toward the door, I belatedly remembered my manners and called back fearfully, "Thank you, sir." Safely at home again, I told Mother than Mr. Porter had laughed at me. She smiled, too, so I was doubly insulted.

I learned just lately that soon after the Civil War, a private school opened in a small wooden building on Porter's Corner. It was taught by Miss Mamie Rush of Blackville, South Carolina, who in time married Dr. Jack Brockington, whose drugstore was on the southwest corner of Main and Academy.

Dr. Jack's widow and their daughter, Mrs. Ada B. Gourdin, and her son, Jack Gourdin, now live on upper Academy Street. Incidentally, that long street was named after the Williamsburg Academy, which flourished during the Reconstruction period. It stood in the present yard of the W.I. Nexsen home at the head of the street.

When Ada, who was an only child, was small, she had a very thick mop of light brown curls and a temper like a firecracker. She got that from Dr. Jack. It was the delight of small boys to enrage her by yelling, "Dr. Jack's rag baby!" after the popular rag dolls with mops of tan knitting wool for hair. Little Ada was still too young to know that boys

Dr. Jack Brockington's pharmacy stood on one corner of the main intersection in Kingstree. *Photograph courtesy of Williamsburgh Historical Museum.*

pick only at girls whose attention they crave, but she learned in plenty of time—as do all females.

Also among the first brick structures in Kingstree was M.F. Heller's Livery and Sales Sables, a portion of which still stands on West Academy, midway the block between Main and Mill Streets, and until recently occupied by Winslow Chevrolet Company.

Many fine horses and mules shipped by railway freight from Missouri and Texas were sold there, in addition to buggies, carriages, surreys with fringe on top and sulkies with long shafts. He also sold democrats, which slightly resembled light pickup trucks. There were one-horse and two-horse wagons, heavy log carts for use in the woods, and handy, two-wheeled road carts which could get through mud holes and deep sand in the roads better than buggies and wagons. The wheels of all vehicles had metal rims, but coming pretty soon were sporty, rubber-tired buggies with narrow hug-me-tight seats to delight courting couples but not their parents. A big corral behind the stables was fenced with stout wooden planks nailed horizontally to the posts. It extended at right angles to the double gates opening on Mill Street.

Mr. Heller was a great-uncle of J.F. "Jack" Arrowsmith and his sister Louise and of J.O. "Picky" Arrowsmith and his sister Mary. Those two pairs are first cousins. The home of Mr. and Mrs. Heller, who had no children,

The Gourdin house on Academy Street has recently been renovated. *Photograph by Linda Brown.*

was in the vast yard on the northwest corner of Academy and Brooks Streets, and it faced the property of the First Baptist Church. A house now in the southern edge of that yard was built years later, as was the house behind it. Jack Arrowsmith's family is now living in the original Heller home.

When Mr. Heller had an artesian well bored in his yard, it brought forth a magnificent gush of soft water, and the overflow had to be piped to an open ditch on Brooks Street. The ditch ran all the way to Black River, which is the western boundary of Kingstree. Small children and their dogs had a fine time playing in that ditch, and for a wonder, nobody drowned.

The town still had no waterworks, so housekeepers had to cope with hand pumps or wells with oaken buckets. Water was heated on black wrought-iron ranges that burned wood. The stoves, while still warm, were wiped daily with wads of newspaper, which left just enough printers' ink to keep iron from rusting.

The privies were built in the back of the vegetable gardens behind all homes. Large gardenia bushes, which were called Cape Jessamines and thrived all over the South, screened the privies from public view, and the overpowering fragrance of their blossoms did practical service.

The Heller house is reported to be the oldest house still standing in Kingstree. *Photograph courtesy of Williamsburgh Historical Museum.*

Modest souls suffered agonies of embarrassment at being seen hurrying down the unscreened paths toward those bushes. Toilet tissue was not yet manufactured, but last year's Sears & Roebuck catalogs had become universal fixtures. Years later, the overall situation spawned the popular wisecrack, "We had a bath and a path."

Of course, there were no bathrooms, so we bathed in tin washtubs in the kitchen, but not with lye soap. When the children in the family weren't too dirty, several had to take turns bathing in the same water. It didn't do the last one any good to gripe about the scum floating on it when his turn came. When the grown-ups bathed, they stuffed paper in the keyholes to keep the children from enjoying a free show. Everybody got a good scrubbing once a week, but the rest of the time, it was a case of washing your face, neck, hands and feet and then "sitting in the basin." Hoyt's German Cologne at ten cents per tiny bottle was a popular perfume—but not if gardenia-scented. No wonder it took Southern belles so long to get over their prejudice against corsages of gardenias. Some still wear them with tongue-in-cheek, and they exchange merry glances with other girls in the know.

Many natives looked askance at Mr. Heller's flowing well and said that the newfangled thing would soon run dry. Others said that it was a sin to "prank with the waters under the Earth." That was God's business. The Negroes said that when the well did run dry, it would leave a great empty space under Heller's Corner. Without the water to hold it up, the dirt would cave in, and the whole corner would drop straight down to Hell, taking that sinner with it.

Material from columns originally published in January 1952, January 1970 and February 1970.

Goose Fights & Mrs. Heller's Parrots

Long ago there was another attraction in the Heller yard. It was a large wire coop for Mrs. Heller's six parrots. Devilish youngsters, including me, liked to play there with Mrs. Heller's niece and namesake, Carrie Scott, who was a redheaded devil in her own right. She and her mother lived with the Hellers.

We delighted in teasing the parrots. They paid no attention if we said, "Shoo," but they couldn't bear hissing sounds. All we had to do was stand innocently near the coop and whisper "Ss-ss-ss" through our teeth, and it wasn't long before every parrot was screaming, "Miss Carrie," as plainly as if they were human. Mrs. Heller, who was a short, plump woman, would come at a trot, often brandishing a long broom of native straw, which was the cue for all of us, including little Carrie, to take to our heels.

Possibly the parrots hated hissing because they hated the great flocks of handsome white geese that roamed the village at will, muttering happily among themselves but hissing at everything and everybody blocking their paths. This included railroad locomotives when it pleased their fancy to cross the track or to take a stroll to the Atlantic Coast Line Railway Station (we called it the depot), which was then a shabby, wooden building in an open field north of town surrounded by farm land, near the present site of the Southern Cities Ice Company. Many geese met their fate there because they never learned that trains wouldn't go around them as people did, especially people wearing white shoes. Even tough little barefoot boys couldn't bear to walk along a squashy goose trail.

One Sunday morning, a group of gentlemen and their ladies was strolling home from the First Baptist Church. There were no cars then. The worshippers were discussing Kingstree's first paved sidewalks (only

Mrs. Carrie Simons Heller. *Photograph courtesy of Gordon B. Jenkinson.*

Main and Academy), of which everybody was very proud. A goose had evidently crossed just ahead of them, but all pretended not to notice, except little Harold Steele, who spoke in a drawl remarkably slow even by Southern standards. "Look, Mama," he said, "an old goose has squirted so-and-so on our pretty new sidewalk." The dead silence was broken by Harold's plaintive, "Mama, don't twist my ear. I didn't do it." Then everybody burst out laughing.

I don't remember seeing any geese hanging around the parrot cage, but as Mrs. Heller owned one of the largest flocks, no doubt they did and hissed plenty. We continued to tease the parrots until we got old enough to be ashamed of ourselves. Then we were glad that Mrs. Heller, who had often given us cookies and lemonade, had never caught on to our meanness. But before we reached that age of decency, we discovered a new variation to our hissing trick. When our excellent teacher, Miss Lorena Ross, was struggling to get the meaning of "apt alliteration's artful aid" through our thick skulls, she also made us memorize this excerpt from Miles Standish: "Silently into the room glided the glistening savage, bearing a serpent's skin and seeming himself like a serpent."

Miss Ross never understood our suddenly awakened interest. Though we still had no idea what alliteration meant, we knew a good thing when we saw it, and most of us memorized the passage quickly, as we knew that we could have fun chanting a classic and tormenting parrots at the same time. To see what I mean, read the quotation very slowly in a loud whisper, giving every "S" a hissing sound. It drove the parrots into a frenzy.

Though geese traveled in large flocks, two flocks seldom met. Apparently they had a system of staking out their own territories, but when two flocks did meet, they put on a battle royal with a noise that was terrific. Small children came running from every direction, gleefully shouting, "Come to the goose fight! Come to the goose fight!" We stopped at a safe distance, but continued to jump up and down with excitement as we watched white feathers flying like a snowstorm.

A fight always stopped suddenly, as if by a secret signal, and the opposing flocks drew apart and ignored each other completely, all mumbling angrily to themselves as they smoothed their ruffled feathers. Then each flock went its separate way, its injured limping along behind, with an occasional broken wing dragging.

Geese hated dogs and vice versa. If a dog ever had his tail clamped in a goose's wide, flat bill, he never troubled one again, but there was many a small circus in the learning. Picture, if you will, a half-grown dog and a full-grown goose fairly well matched as to weight, fastened bill-to-tail whirling around like a merry-go-round, the dog yapping bloody murder, the goose's wings flapping for balance, its yellow, webbed feet touching the ground now and then for leverage. Imagine other dogs barking wildly, other geese honking wildly, children screaming wildly, the owner of the dog weeping wildly. Which side won depended entirely upon your point of view. The goose tired first and let go the tail, but it was always the dog that fled the scene of battle.

When a goose was completely outweighed by the dog, there was no whirling around. The dog took off at full speed, howling with pain and terror, the goose with wings outspread, towed like a glider behind him. Everything got out of their way. The goose always gave up first and turned the tail loose. Then the goose hung around a bit, grumbling to himself as he smoothed his feathers. But the dog was gone for good!

Material from columns originally published in February 1970.

Children Playing

In the old days, nearly every yard in Kingstree had shade trees for young children to climb, some with wooden slats nailed like ladders against the trunks. From some hung long rope swings of which we never tired, two of us standing face to face on a slat for a seat and pumping 'til we soared halfway to heaven, or so we thought.

There was ample space for other games without number. Nobody had ever heard of organized playgrounds, and children created their own entertainment, playing together and settling their own occasional battles.

We played baseball with shingles for bats and balls made of string. We fished with wild onion stems in tiny doodle holes in spots bare of grass. We could really catch those doodles, which some people called "jacks." I don't know why we didn't try eating them, unless it was because they were so ugly. We turned them loose to go and sin no more, but the witless things would bite the next stems poked into their holes and cling 'til pulled to the surface again. Maybe they liked onions.

In midsummer we climbed big mulberry trees and perched on the spreading limbs to feast on luscious purple berries shaped like fat caterpillars and bursting with extremely sweet juice. The heady aroma perfumed the air around us. We had been warned repeatedly that mulberries were inhabited, but if they were, the inhabitants were purple, too, so they didn't bother us. I now suspect that we were warned because mulberry stains were so hard to remove from our clothes.

The strip of woods bordering Black River, which bounds Kingstree on the west, was teeming with foxes, deer, rabbits, squirrels, opossums (which we called 'possums) and raccoons (which we called 'coons). When a 'possum was threatened by an enemy on the warpath, he collapsed on the ground and played dead, not moving a muscle 'til his enemy had walked

Kingstree's streets and yards are even today shaded by numerous ancient oak trees. *Photograph by Linda Brown.*

Black River has recently been designated as a scenic river. *Photograph by Linda Brown.*

indifferently away. The long fingers on the 'coons' front paws were a delight to children, for they made the paws look like comical black hands, and those fingers could do nearly everything ours could.

In the woods by the river there were wild turkeys, ducks, geese, cranes, herons, turtles and egrets that grew beautiful aigrette plumes. There were also huge bullfrogs, called swamp chickens because when their long hind legs were cooked, they had the delicate flavor of fried chicken. We children couldn't bear to look at the gruesome things—much less eat them—after learning that the muscles contracted when placed in hot fat, making the legs kick like mad 'til they finally gave up in despair, resigned to being eaten.

Material from columns originally published in February 1970.

Wild Horses in the Street

L ong ago there wasn't a paved sidewalk, much less a paved street, in Kingstree.

It was well the big front yards were enclosed in white picket fences for us young fry to hang over as we watched the activities of livestock rambling around at will.

The incomparable thrill for us was when word spread by grapevine telegraph (we had never seen a telephone) that two or three boxcars of wild horses from Texas or Missouri would be unloaded shortly. They were on the Atlantic Coast Line siding, near the old, wooden railroad station, which we called the depot, about a mile north of town.

Mothers hastened to collect offspring and trekked to various piazzas, which would provide grandstand views of the parade on its way down long Academy Street to M.F. Heller's Livery and Sales Stables, which were centered a block into the business district. The big L-shaped corral, which we called the lot, behind them had sturdy double gates opening on a side street.

The star of the show was a tall, lanky youth with straight, black hair, merry brown eyes and a gift of gab. Otis Arrowsmith was later to become a state legislator, but then he was working for his prosperous uncle, M.F. Heller, a town character if I ever saw one, who owned the stables. As Otis expressed it, he was "Uncle Mike's stable boy and the horses' chambermaid."

Children adored Otis, who was never in too much of a hurry for a word with us. Better still, he never disagreed with us, and anything we said or did was absolutely right—our parents just didn't know what they were talking about.

The said parents didn't think as highly of Otis as we did. He was the one person in our lives, then or later, who told us only what we wanted to hear, the truth having nothing to do with the case.

This view, looking north on Academy Street, shows the white picket fences that enclosed yards early in the last century. *Photograph courtesy of Williamsburgh Historical Museum.*

It was Otis's responsibility to get the new horses from the depot to Mr. Heller's lot, so at the appointed time, he mounted a beautiful white steed whose long tail almost touched the ground and he went at a leisurely cantor to the siding. There, he stopped a short distance opposite the unloading chutes and calmly waited, his own horse's head toward town.

Presently, Tom Mitchell and Will Graham, who had worked years for Mr. Heller, opened the boxcar doors and fanned the wild stock out—with their hats, by gum!

The instant the first excited horse emerged, his eyes rolling wildly, business picked up. Otis gave a loud, attention-drawing whoop, touched his heels to his own steed and was off like a streak, his horse's tail a long, white streamer behind him, the back of Otis's white shirt billowing like a sail in the wind.

One by one the new horses hit the ground running and took off at full speed after the white horse. For reasons unknown to me, they would not follow the lead of a dark horse.

Every few moments, Otis, who could pitch his deep voice like a foghorn, threw a quick glance behind him and bawled, "Cope, cope!" Don't ask me what "cope" meant. I don't know, but those crazed animals did.

They followed Otis, who was crouched low over his saddle, as if their lives depended on catching up with him. Down the unpaved streets they pounded, dust and mud flying, squawking fowls fluttering right and left, dogs yelping in frenzy.

"Cope," bayed Otis to the tune of flying hoofbeats, only interrupting his call to choke on laughter when he chanced to see one of his own cronies skedaddling to safety.

The new stock followed the flying streak until it led them straight through the big gates that slammed shut behind them. Only then did they realize they had been corralled. Some tried to kick the wooden fences down, but things were built for permanence in the good old days.

Looking back, I marvel that nobody got killed or maimed. Was it expert human organization or the grace of the Lord? Pure luck could not have held so consistently.

The fact that it was also Otis's responsibility to break his Uncle Mike's new horses to harness before they could be offered for sale daunted him not a whit. Nobody had ever seen an automobile in this agricultural area. Horses played a big part in the way of life, not only of farmers, but of townspeople as well. Most men were good judges of horseflesh, and horse swapping was the order of the day.

At times, when extra-fine animals were involved, the moves were as slow, skillful and tedious as a game of chess in the hands of experts—and lasted as long. Often bets made at the outset were raised as time went by, a secret carefully kept from wives who disapproved of betting.

Both trading and betting were strictly honest. If a man's word wasn't his bond, that individual was held at a distance by responsible men. But pity the slick stranger who appeared from nowhere and let it be known he had a few horses he wouldn't mind parting with. Then there were no holds barred. If occasionally the stranger managed to outsmart the local lights, that gave them something to rehash for months to come and better prepared them to fleece the next traveling crook before he could fleece them.

In those leisurely days, nobody was in a hurry, so Otis, Tom and Will tackled the job of breaking the new stock one by one. First, a horse was lassoed in the lot in which no children were allowed. Then he was blindfolded and a bridle put on him, which was in itself no small achievement.

Once the men had managed to hitch the horse to a light vehicle (I think it was called a sulky, and now I'm wondering if the name had anything to do with the horse's attitude) he was led through the big gates to the side street where children waited on fences, banister railings, rooftops and in trees, depending on age and sex. There the blindfold was removed and the show was on.

The black sulky glistened like polished patent leather, and its two wheels were bright red but had no rubber tires; they were to appear a few years later. Also, it had extra-long shafts. A horse, wild with fright, could kick all he pleased, but his flailing heels could not reach the sulky behind him, nor

Otis, who was perched on the narrow seat that had no back. If, at times, the excited animal's gyrations succeeded in upsetting the vehicle, Otis was expecting just that and landed lightly on his feet, still holding the reins and still talking in soothing monotones to the frightened beast.

Occasionally, when Otis used a long buggy whip on a trembling foam-flecked horse, we chicken-hearted little girls wept and silently prayed to the Lord above to let the horse kick our adored Otis into the middle of next week, or else bite his head off. But we prayed with eyes wide open, still watching in horror 'til the exhausted beast was conquered by man and began obeying his master's will.

Children are quick to forgive, and when we yelled, "Goodbye, Otis," he gave us the high sign but didn't look back. We yelled goodbyes in turn to Tom and Will, who favored us with waves and broad smiles as they headed back to the corral. Tom, who called every child "Baby," shouted, "You-all can come out and play now, Babies!"

Will added, "But you-all had better play on the sidewalk. The new horse will be back to-reckly."

Material from columns originally published in November 1964.

M.F. Heller & the Loafers' Paradise

It now surprises me when I look back to those days long ago and realize that the lives of so many people of all ages in Kingstree and Williamsburg County were affected by activities connected with M.F. Heller's Livery and Sales Stables.

Mr. Heller himself was an enigma. A very small man with no claim to good looks, he was popular with most other men, but some women despised him and didn't care who knew it. However, it was said openly that Mr. Heller's great interest in beautiful horses was exceeded only by his greater interest in women, beautiful and otherwise.

I remember Mr. Heller as far back as I can remember anything, and I knew him 'til he died of old age, but I still don't feel qualified to judge him fairly. I do know that he was a gracious host in his own home and never appeared to tire of dispensing hospitality there. I believe, too, that he was a kind and generous man, but like the rest of us, he had his faults and some drew adverse public criticism, which never seemed to disturb him in the least.

Mr. Heller's business offices occupied only one front corner of his sprawling building in the heart of town, and the rest of the wide frontage on Academy Street was called Loafers' Paradise, where good liquor was free at all times. It was a sort of rough club for men, and I don't mean a club for rough men, for the womanless haven seemed to draw like the proverbial magnet. It was haphazardly furnished with easy chairs and cots. There were also tables for card games that reputedly never ended, new players merely replacing those who dropped out or passed out. The reading material included the Charleston *News and Courier*, the oldest daily newspaper in the South, and a sensational magazine called the *Police Gazette*. On the walls there were pictures of beautiful horses, as well as beautiful women,

One of Kingstree's early baseball teams. M.F. Heller is on the far left in the third row. *Photograph courtesy of W.E Jenkinson III.*

Academy Street during the time Heller's Livery Stable was a focal point of the town. *Photograph courtesy of Williamsburgh Historical Museum.*

the latter—which left nothing to the imagination—were said to have been painted by tramp artists passing through town.

Of course, bits of bawdy man-talk trickled out every now and then, and many women grew to hate the place. Some would walk around the block rather than pass those windows and be given the speculative once-over by some of the gentlemen who might be lounging inside.

The wives of some farmers complained that their husbands would not have traded horses nor bought new ones they could ill afford if they hadn't been full of free liquor, but some of their friends opined that certain husbands got full of liquor anyway, so why blame Mr. Heller.

Other ladies complained that Mr. Heller spent too much of his idle time on the sidewalk outside his building, where he sat for hours in a straight chair tilted back against the brick wall. There he not only watched the world go by, but studied every female from top to toe as thoroughly as if she were a filly up for auction.

However, Mr. Heller himself claimed that such was only an unfortunate habit of his, that he was really beginning to feel his age and could no longer see very well. When the ladies heard that, they said he was a champion Ananias with lust in his eyes and that he was an evil-minded old goat besides and that he made them sick.

Of course, such remarks were eventually repeated to Mr. Heller, who only shook with laughter and continued to sit on the sidewalk, often with several other loafers keeping him company or helping him look—take your choice.

During my childhood, Mr. Heller was always kind and polite to me, but, to tell the truth, things did seem to change a little after I grew up. There were times then that I, too, squirmed under some of his speculative glances, which didn't seem to miss a trick. Nor did the glances appear to me those of an elderly gentleman who was having trouble with failing eyesight. But who knows?

Material from columns originally published in March 1970.

Editor's note: This story was not published when Bessie Swann Britton's columns first appeared in the *County Record* in the 1950s. Here is her explanation: "After writing the series long ago, I crossed out several stories and some details of others lest their earthy language offend delicate sensibilities. However, when I recently began copying the original manuscript, which had become too dim and brittle with age for the printers to handle, I had second thoughts. Life itself is not always in good taste. The object of the stories in the first place was to try to preserve a true record of the everyday doings in an era long past. So, I decided to publish the facts as I then remembered them, and I beg to be forgiven if the language of those times offends anyone. I don't have to tell you that I am not a professional writer. I'm just a scribbler of sorts, but to keep the memories of early days from being lost forever, I suppose my scribblings will have to do 'til a professional comes along."

Pretty Ladies in Pink Frills

One day long ago, a group of small girls had managed somehow to escape detection, and we were having a fine time playing in the forbidden territory at the corral behind M.F. Heller's Livery and Sales Stables. My little sister Eula Swann and her constant playmate, Claudia Jones, had tagged along with me and Alice McConnell, Miriam Fluitt, Tyson McFadden and a Colored child named Lula. Even small boys had strict orders from their parents to stay away from the stables and corral under penalty of having their little britches dusted, but the activities at both places were so irresistible that the boys often took their punishment rather than miss the fun.

As for little girls, we didn't have a chance. Not only would our parents have skinned us for going to the stables, all the men working there kept a sharp watch to shoo us away if we even rambled too near. We often wished for some magic to turn us into boys.

It was Otis Arrowsmith who discovered us at the corral, and that was the only time I ever saw him angry. We had recently seen our first Barnum & Bailey Circus, and its wonders had given us new ideas. We had been most impressed by the pretty ladies with pink frills walking tightropes high in the air and by a hideous elephant named "Mom."

The high fence around the corral had stout wooden planks nailed crosswise with cracks between them just right for climbing, and when Otis discovered us, everyone was walking barefoot on the narrow top edge of the fence. We were paying no attention whatsoever to a magnificent black stallion inside the corral, prancing and snorting restively just a few feet from us.

Alice and I were the oldest in the group and Eula, Claudia and Lula the youngest, but none was old enough to have bat-brains, so none knew the difference between a killer stallion and a harmless plowhorse.

We liked all horses. They had been a part of our lives since the day we were born, and we had no fear of them. Of course, we knew that some horses would kick if they got mad with you, but we also knew that they could kick only with their hind feet, so we never stood behind one. And we had seen horses accidentally step on venturesome kittens and puppies, so we knew never to go under a horse's belly. Also, we knew that a runaway horse would run over crazy people who didn't get out of its way, but we weren't crazy. Too, we had often seen horses bite each other, but we knew also that horses didn't eat children. So why should we be afraid of horses?

We were still indifferent to the stallion pawing nearby when Otis, speaking with forced calm, told us to see who could jump the farthest at the same time to the grass outside the corral. We knew we had done wrong, and we were feeling too uneasy to tell him that we had never before jumped off anything that high. Besides, we were used to taking orders without argument. We were like Tennyson's Immortal Six Hundred, "Ours not to reason why, ours but to do and die." So, off we sprang. Our luck was better than theirs, for all landed safely with only Eula, Claudia and Lula whimpering to go home.

Ordinarily, Otis would have taken time to comfort them. Instead, he exploded wrathfully, and demanded to know what in the devil we had been doing on that fence. We meekly explained that we were pretty ladies with pink frills walking on a high rope. Otis didn't even smile. He just said he would be goddamned. After a moment, he angrily added that if he told our mothers where we had been, we would be pretty ladies with pink bottoms, and that we would sure as heck be walking on something or other, because when they got through with us, we wouldn't be able to sit down for a week. And furthermore, if we ever came back to that corral that he himself would give everyone of us a good thrashing with a long buggy whip.

But Otis didn't tell. Needless to say, we didn't, either. And we older children made it very clear to poor little Eula, Claudia and Lula, who were by then sniffling pitifully, what we would do to them if they ever told. They never did—so nobody ever got pinked for that escapade.

Dead Horses in the Bone Yard

L ong ago, every yard had a picket fence to keep children in and the freely roving livestock out. Even in the old days boys had some freedom, but we little girls couldn't go out of sight of our own front doors without permission.

We had never seen a moving picture, much less a horror movie, but horror seemed to hold a fascination for children even then. Little girls longed to visit a gruesome place called the Bone Yard, to which dead horses and cows were dragged and left without burial a few miles across Black River, which borders the town. We didn't have a chance; only boys had that much freedom.

One hot afternoon, two venturesome little brothers named Royal and Barney Flowers swaggered slowly along our street and deigned to pause a moment to watch a group of small girls playing hopscotch under a large, moss-draped oak in our yard. Royal, who was older, called to us that they had been to the Bone Yard, and asked if we wanted to hear about it. We did. All raced to the fence and listened greedily.

You could smell the Bone Yard a mile away, boasted little Barney—two if luck was with you and the wind was blowing your way. There were a thousand dead horses, mules and cows—both brothers crossed their hearts and hoped to die—and a million big black buzzards "tearing and gobbling them up." When a buzzard couldn't hold any more, he upchucked and started over, time and again, until every bone was clean and white, and all the meat was gone.

We were so entranced by the mental picture the brothers finally left with us that we again tried to kiss our elbows, for we believed that to be the only sure way to turn girls into boys who could go where they pleased and hobnob with buzzards. Girls could never get even a close look a buzzard.

All we could do was lie on the grass and watch the great birds gliding and wheeling so high and peep into the huge nests and see the baby buzzards while they were still white, but not even Royal dared to steal one because the mama buzzard would pick his eyes out and feed them to her babies.

We decided that it was either the hot sun that soon turned the buzzards black or else the devil himself didn't like them because they enjoyed playing jump rope in the Bone Yard.

We were used to seeing an occasional dead animal dragged by our home en route to the Bone Yard, but one day as we were happily skipping our own ropes, we saw a dead saddle horse we had known personally. His name was Prince, and we recognized his familiar markings, notwithstanding the fact that his neck was stretched nearly twice its normal length by the stout chain looped around it and fastened to the back of a heavy log cart drawn by two powerful mules.

We wondered what had kept the chain from pulling Prince's head off, and though we had admired him greatly, if bad had come to worse, we hoped to be present. We had seen fowls and pigs without their heads and had studied pictures of kings and queens who had lost theirs, not to mention a highly colored painting in the big family Bible of no man at all, just his head on a platter like Mama used when serving tea to callers in the parlor, but we had never seen any headless thing as big as a horse.

A giant of a black man named Sambo, known to us personally, and one of our favorites of many Negro friends, was driving the mules. When we yelled for him to stop and let us put some flowers on Prince, he threw back his head with a shout of laughter and willingly obliged.

We ran to the garden for clusters of yellow chrysanthemums blooming in profusion and stuck one in each link of the chain around Prince's neck. Sambo admired them and asked that we put some in the band of his old felt hat, greasy and dirty and perched on his thick mop of dusty hair, which hadn't been sheared in weeks. We were happy to oblige and helped him yank his hat one way and then the other to get the prettiest effect. Finally we told him he looked beautiful; we believed it and so did he.

He cautioned us to be careful getting down off the cart because if the mules took a notion (you never could tell about fool mules) to start with a jerk, we might fall under the wheels, which would mash us flatter than fritters, and he would have to come back and scoop us up with a shovel and haul us to the Bone Yard, which might make him late going to see his gal that night.

As we got down carefully, we asked why Prince's tongue hung out so long, and Sambo said it had talked too much. He drove off chuckling, leaving us to speculate as to how one horse knew what another was saying, and also why a dead horse looked so swollen. It must have been something he ate, we decided, like too many green oats, which could kill a horse.

Presently we dismissed the whole thing and returned to our rope skipping. In the distance we could hear Sambo's rich baritone. He liked crazy songs that made other people on the street laugh with him. We began chanting, too, for we knew every one of the many verses, and we timed our skips to their easy beat.

Material from columns originally published in March 1965.

Paying Social Calls

Long ago, it was the custom in Kingstree for a mother occasionally to take a little daughter with her when paying a social call in the afternoon. That was to let the little dressed-up victim practice doing the correct things in polite society. Every little daughter loathed the custom. The last thing she wanted was to behave correctly anywhere.

Before leaving home, the little girl was reminded that children should be seen but not heard. She must remember to say, "Thank you, ma'am," if the hostess or a maid served refreshments. She must eat the refreshments with relish, whether she liked them or not, but must leave a little food on her plate and never take second helpings.

She was not to chew with her mouth open and must use her napkin when needed. If no refreshments were served, she was not to make some excuse to go to the kitchen to see what was cooking there. She must speak only when spoken to, but never ask questions. She must sit still in her chair, but never sit spraddle-legged. She must not pick her nose and must not scratch no matter where she itched. Also, she must remember when leaving to bow sweetly to the hostess and thank her for such a lovely time.

One of my closest friends in grammar school was a dainty little fireball with shoulder-length black curls. She was named Frances Denmark Sullivan, only daughter of the late Mr. and Mrs. J.T. Sullivan. She was two years older than I but was small for her age.

She claimed that she had learned to fight like a wildcat because her younger brothers, Walter and James, liked to double-team her. She had never liked the name Frances, and she despised Denmark, so at school she always gave her name as Fannie D. Sullivan. Once when a teacher insisted on knowing what "D" stood for, Fannie told her "Devil," adding demurely that it was an old family name. The teacher, thinking it was one of those unfortunate names sometimes handed down for generations, entered only the initial, while Fannie smiled like the cat that had eaten the canary.

A game popular with small children was called hail-over, which meant, "Look out, a baseball is coming over." Half the players took their stands on one side of a one-story outbuilding or a kitchen, which extended back from the main body of a big dwelling such as most people had in those days of cheap land, cheap lumber and cheap labor. As a player hurled the ball over the building, he yelled, "Hail-over," and the players on the other side raced to see who could catch the ball before it hit the ground. Whoever caught the ball would hurl it back with the same yell. I don't remember how points were counted in the game.

One summer afternoon, Mrs. Sullivan went to call on Mrs. H.O. Britton. Fannie was dressed in starched white organdy trimmed with lace. A wide, pink satin ribbon was tied around her middle and a matching bow perched on top of her dark curls. Unfortunately, the visitors arrived just as the three little Britton brothers, Harry, John and Billie (W.J.), were all set to go to a neighbor's to play.

Mrs. Britton told her sons that they must be her "little gentlemen" and stay home to entertain their guest, but they could play outdoors if they would let the guest choose the game. Fannie innocently chose to play hail-over. With the ladies safely indoors having afternoon tea and cakes, the ball teams shaped up. The brothers were on one side and the guest on the other, the brothers holding the ball. Fannie was a good catcher, and when she heard "Hail-over," she ran full speed ahead and caught the ball, but the ball turned out to be a small brickbat. By the time the smoke had cleared, the brothers were long gone, but when hunger drove them home that night, they got their just desserts. Fortunately, Fannie suffered no serious injury, but she had lost all taste for the Britton brothers.

Material from columns originally published in June 1970.

Two Houses

This story is about the home of the late Dr. and Mrs. D.C. Scott on Railroad Avenue, where every house once had a flower garden that was a showplace. Several generations before I was born, Mrs. Scott's mother, who was the wife of Dr. John Brockinton, went to call on her sister, Mrs. R.C. Logan, whose imposing home was at the head of Hampton Avenue. I don't know where Mrs. Brockinton was living at the time.

Shortly before the visit, Mrs. Logan had bought a Currier & Ives print titled "American Country Life," which featured a large residence with beautifully proportioned lines. It was hanging over the mantelpiece in Mrs. Logan's parlor. The visitor studied the print several moments in silent admiration, and then solemnly declared, "Someday I'm going to build a house like that." And she did.

The Logan house has a comical history all its own. Many years earlier, when Mr. R.C. Logan was getting ready to build the house, he placed an order with a small sawmill for some of the material, including massive foundation timbers. The mill wasn't equipped to handle such a big order, but the owner, who needed the business, hated to admit it. Knowing he couldn't change his mill's capacity, he decided that his only hope was to change his customer's requirements. If he could persuade Mr. Logan to build a small house, his small mill could supply the material. So, he wrote Mr. Logan a long letter in the flowery language of the day and protested the building of such a large mansion on earth. He recommended instead that Mr. Logan devote his efforts toward a mansion in heaven where "neither moth nor rust doth corrupt, nor thieves break through and steal."

At first, Mr. Logan was rocked back on his heels by the letter, which his family has preserved to this day, but he later replied in equally flowery language that it was his ambition to build mansions in both places. Mr. Logan

R.C. Logan not only founded *The County Record*, but also served as Clerk of Court for Williamsburg County. *Photograph courtesy of Williamsburgh Historical Museum.*

got his supplies from a big mill, whose successful owner has been forgotten, but the struggling owner of the small mill will be long remembered.

That was the first flattop house in Williamsburg County, and it was quite a departure from the traditional homes hereabouts. Besides, it was painted a bright bluish-gray instead of the traditional white. The house was so sensational that people came from distant places to visit it.

The Italianate-style Logan house drew many visitors in its day. *Photograph courtesy of Williamsburgh Historical Museum.*

One day, a tall, elderly Negro with snowy white hair came from one of the outlying plantations to take a look. When he first beheld the blue mansion glistening in the bright sunlight, he stopped in his tracks and stared in silent awe. Then he took off his hat and bowed low to the house. He stood bareheaded several moments, staring mutely at the glory before him. Finally, the old man clasped his hands as if in prayer and exclaimed with devout reverence, "Behold, King Solomon's temple!"

I don't know who first got tired of the blue color, but the Logan house has been white ever since I can remember it.

Editor's note: Sadly, neither of these two homes is still standing.

Old Town vs. New Town

In 1732, a man appeared on a street in Boston, Massachusetts, holding a black cotton umbrella over his head. That was the first umbrella ever seen in the United States. It made horses run away, spilling passengers from cabs and carriages. Small boys had fun throwing things at the strange object, and made the man run away. However, umbrellas were here to stay. In time, dainty silk parasols in pastel colors, edged with frills and lace, "covered Dixie like the dew."

The only person I ever saw carrying a frilled model was Miss Florence Hirsch, who was a young lady when I was a small child. At that time there were only three houses between the First Baptist Church on that side of Academy Street and Highway No. 52: the old Gilland home on the northeast corner of Academy and Kelley Streets, the old Brockington home where the W.I. Nexsen house now stands, and the old Hirsch home, which is still standing at 316 W. Academy Street and is now owned by Mr. and Mrs. (Wylma McCollough) W.J. Green.

Across the street, there was only one house between the Williamsburg Presbyterian Church on upper Academy Street and Highway No. 52. That was known as the old Grayson house and was later bought by Mr. and Mrs. Dozier Burgess and is now owned by their daughter, Mrs. Alvena Tomlinson of Olanta. All the Graysons are gone, and of that branch of the Burgess family, only Mr. and Mrs. (Sallie Bartell) Keels Burgess and Mr. and Mrs. (Ruby Bartell) Leonard Burgess still live in Kingstree. Those Burgess brothers married Bartell sisters from the Indiantown community.

Many of you were kind to Miss Florence Hirsch in her last years. After she had outlived the rest of her family, she sold their old home and moved downtown to the house that is now my home on the southwest corner of Church and Academy Streets. When Miss Florence was still a young lady,

This house, one of the oldest in Kingstree, was the first built in an area later known as "New Town." *Photograph courtesy of Williamsburgh Historical Museum.*

the only dwelling north of Kelley Street, which was then a dirt road, was the house now owned by Mrs. Elise K. Hodges and Mr. and Mrs. (Margaret Hodges) Marc Hauenstein at 506 Live Oak Avenue.

In time, that section, which had been dense woods and cultivated fields, was cut into half-acre lots, and the town limits were extended to include them. A feud of sorts sprang up between boys living in New Town and boys in Old Town. Nobody had automobiles then, and a young sport who dared go on foot out of his own territory to escort a girl to a dance knew he was safe only 'til he had returned the girl to her home. Then he knew to run for his life, zigzagging to dodge the barrage of small rocks and brickbats aimed at his legs by enemies in the dark.

Though such hazards chilled the ardor of a few timid lads, most kept going back for more. Maybe the ordeals helped the braver lads to develop social poise. It did take poise for a fellow to appear carefree at a dance, knowing what was ahead of him. He couldn't even look forward to a goodnight kiss on the girl's porch for fear his lurking enemies would kill him there. Nor did he dare step inside her front door for fear her father would kill him there. But love has always found a way, and in time a few Old Town boys married New Town girls and vice versa.

I think the late J.W. Coward built the first house on Kelley Street. That house at 302 is now owned by Mr. and Mrs. (Lillian Woodham) Leroy Payne. Their daughters, Frances, Eloise, Lina May (who is called Peepsie) and Lillian (Tumpy) had the good luck to inherit their mother's lovely complexion. Once when Peepsie was about five and cute as a doll, she thought she was due to get a spanking, so she hid in the shrubbery by the porch. When her mother opened the door and called, "Peepsie, where are you?" Peepsie answered, "I'm away off yonder—somewhere in a big field." She didn't get the spanking.

Material from columns originally published in September 1970.

Fire!

L ong ago, when I was a child in Kingstree, people used kerosene lamps, wood-burning stoves and open fireplaces. There was no metal or composition roofing, so all buildings were covered with wooden shingles, which in time became dry as tinder. There were no waterworks and no fire department—only volunteer bucket brigades. Fire was public enemy number one.

Recently, Edward C. Welch showed me a fire map of Kingstree made in 1909 by the Sanborn Map Company of New York City. It gave the population as 1,800, which was probably a euphemistic figure, as there were no industries in this agricultural area, and the majority of families lived on their outlying farms.

The map shows the location of "three underground cisterns, each with a capacity of 30,000 gallons of water from driven wells, natural flow." One was at the intersection of Main and Academy streets, where the Confederate Monument once stood. One was at the intersection of Main and Jackson Streets. (Jackson was then called Jail Street.) The other was near the front boundary of the lot on the southeast corner of Academy and Mill Streets, now the site of Hugh D. Gamble's Modern Service Station.

Apparently there were no cisterns in the residential areas. The map showed that Kingstree then had "one hand-drawn fire engine with a bell on the engine but no hose cart and no hook-and-ladder conveyance."

A similar map made in 1913 gave the population as 2,000 and said, "fire alarms are given by ringing church bells." I don't know why the maps were made unless they had something to do with fire insurance rates.

In time, artesian wells were bored at various points all over town, but the water wasn't used for fires, so it's likely that the town then had a fire department and waterworks. Year after year, each artesian well brought

The Williamsburg Presbyterian Church. *Photograph courtesy of Williamsburgh Historical Museum.*

forth about a two-inch flow of soft water that poured without ceasing into stationary horse troughs, from which it was piped into nearby Black River.

Our village really came to life when anybody began screaming "Fire!" in the night. Everybody in hearing distance echoed the scream and all rushed outside half-clad to see if their own roofs were safe before rushing to join the bucket brigade helping the other fellow. Volunteers could cope with fires when small, but they could only watch helplessly while big ones burned themselves out.

There were no automobiles, but most homes had stables behind them. Horses had to be blindfolded and led to safety, as it was said that a large fire caused horses to panic, and some would dash into a fire instead of running from it.

Heavy bells in the tall towers of three wooden churches—Methodist, Baptist and Presbyterian—on upper Academy Street were rung to alarm the countryside. A coarse Manila rope hung from each bell to the vestibule floor. Just calling back to mind the sudden discordant clamor of those loud bells in the night still makes goose bumps come on me, or perhaps it was only that being small, I lost my sense of security at seeing grown-ups in a bewildered state of fear.

However, life has a way of providing a bit of comic relief for mortals, even when threatened by tragedy. Let me tell you about the Colored sextons who were employed to keep the bells ringing as long as a fire lasted. At first,

The Kingstree United Methodist Church. *Photograph courtesy of Williamsburgh Historical Museum.*

The Kingstree First Baptist Church can be seen at the far left of this view down Brooks Street. *Photograph courtesy of Williamsburgh Historical Museum.*

the sextons, like everybody else, were wild with excitement, but if the blaze lasted long enough for them to settle into stride, they instinctively began to improvise ragtime tunes on those bells. That was something worth hearing.

It was the duty of certain church officers to awaken the sextons when fire broke out at night. On Sundays, the sextons who took their responsibility seriously enjoyed ringing the church bells slowly and with perfect timing to call worshipers to services, but ringing to alarm the countryside was another story. The updraft from the heat of a burning building could send blazing shingles hurtling through space to land on other dry roofs a block away. All possible manpower was needed for the small blazes before it was too late.

With every restraint removed, those sextons with rhythm in their bones had the time of their lives. For them it was like an answer to prayer. They threw their full weight on the coarse ropes and went to town. The air pulsated with sound as they tried to outdo each other in volume, striving at the same time to synchronize the clamor of their bells, as carpenters on a building job will sometimes synchronize the rat-a-tat-tat of their hammers. Clang-clangity-clang! (Methodist), Clung, clungity, clung! (Baptist), Clong, clingity, clong! (Presbyterian). Presently all the bells were swinging together in joyful harmony. A new ragtime tune was born.

Material from columns originally published in October 1970.

Fire in the Night

Throughout my own childhood, the village had no fire department, only stationary cisterns from which bucket brigades carried water by hand to fight small blazes before they became disasters. Mr. and Mrs. J.C. Kinder and children lived in a white frame dwelling on the northwest corner of Academy and Mill Streets. Mr. and Mrs. Hugh McCutchen had recently moved from Indiantown to a similar house next door. They had no children, but years later, Mrs. McCutchen's orphaned young niece, Dorothy Dobbin, made her home with them, and she still lives here. Also, years later, a son of Mr. and Mrs. Thomas McCutchen was named for his uncle, and that Hugh McCutchen still lives here.

One night it was discovered that the McCutchen roof was blazing. At the dreaded scream, "FIRE," half-clad people appeared from nowhere, some to run around in circles echoing the scream.

Mrs. Kinder recalls that Mr. McCutchen, who she said was prematurely gray, stood on his front porch, his nightshirt flapping in the breeze, loudly shouting, "Water! Water! For God's sake, bring us water!"

As if in answer to his prayer, the bucket brigade came at a trot. Some had water buckets, some had milk pails with built-in strainers, some had small tubs used nightly to wash their feet, some had big tubs used on Monday morning to wash their clothes and used on Saturday night to wash themselves. Everybody's dogs were barking wildly.

Pretty soon the Colored sextons got on the job, ringing the bells at the three churches to alarm the countryside that help was needed. After a few false starts, the sextons got into stride and the bells pealed forth full strength, adding their joyful medley to the confusion already rampant.

In the meantime, things were happening in the big two-story frame house across the street from the fire. The family of J.P. Adams lived downstairs,

Kingstree finally got a fire wagon, which won a prize in Orangeburg. The prize was the horse seen to the right in the photo. *Photograph courtesy of Williamsburgh Historical Museum.*

while the upper floor was occupied by Mr. Sam F. Epps and family. Mr. Epps was the grandfather of Mildred Dennis, now Mrs. Willard Wheeler.

For some reason, Mr. Adams was slow in waking up, but as he cleared the front steps with one leap, he felt the need for drastic action, so he whipped out his trusty .44 and began firing it into the air. The five Epps children who had been awakened by the commotion were too young to go to the fire, but they were hanging over the banisters in their porch upstairs to see what they could see.

But they hadn't looked for hot bullets to singe their hair. All five fell back screaming. Luckily, nobody got perforated by the bullets, although Mr. Epps, who was usually a very mild man, did threaten to perforate Mr. Adams. But the words with which Mrs. (Carrie Smith) Adams blasted her husband only singed his hair and eyebrows.

Mrs. (Marguerite Flagler) Kinder can't recall whether the McCutchen house was destroyed, but she does remember that the intense heat blistered her house next door. The bucket brigade kindly washed cold water against her windowpanes and great was the popping thereof.

Material from columns originally published in November 1970.

Spying Shamelessly

When we were growing up in Kingstree, it had no picture shows, no comic books, no library and no organized games. In fact, children were supposed to be "seen and not heard," so we had to create our own diversions. One of our favorite pastimes was keeping up with the romances in town, just as if they were continued stories.

Many adults would have been astonished to learn how much we knew of their activities. Younger brothers and sisters, nieces and nephews spied shamelessly upon courting couples who had no cars for rambling but made pretty good time in hammocks on vine-screened porches and on parlor sofas with kerosene lamps turned low, and the spies obligingly kept other little demons posted on the developments.

Most of us were being reared by principles of honor, but we didn't consider such delightful entertainment dishonorable if we didn't get caught and didn't tell any grown-ups what we knew. Or perhaps that was the instinct of self-preservation, for it was the custom in the good old days to apply the switch first and the questions second.

We were always delighted when lovers made up after a quarrel, and sometimes we knew of engagements before they were officially announced.

P.H. Stoll, who was then a handsome young attorney, was one of our star performers. Perhaps you know him only as a dignified retired judge, ex-solicitor, and ex-congressman, but we "knew him when." Recently, when I asked permission to take his name in vain in this column, Judge Stoll graciously consented but said he "never was much of a ladies' man." But I was like the fellow on Fibber McGee's radio program who always says, "That ain't the way I heard it."

Mr. Stoll had a good voice, and often on summer nights he was among the group of young people harmonizing on somebody's front porch. Now, when I see the judge impeccably groomed, as always, and carrying his dapper cane as he takes his dignified stroll by our house, I find it hard to believe I ever heard him singing lustily, "Rufus Rastus Johnson Brown, What you gonna do when the rent comes 'round?"

However, Mr. Stoll gave us romantic-minded youngsters the surprise of our lives by marrying a girl we didn't even know. We waited eagerly for our first glimpse of Miss Evelyn Cunningham of Indiantown, and only when we had unanimously pronounced her lovely and sweet did the marriage receive our unsolicited blessing.

We were still interested when the popular couple's first child was born, and several went (uninvited) to see the new baby. Annie Baker (now Mrs. G.E. Beatty) and I went together, and that was the first time I ever saw Philip C. Stoll, Esq. He was a beautiful baby. (Philip, I haven't said you aren't beautiful now, but I'll have to admit you don't look much like that little angel cooing in his fluffy white blanket.)

Material from columns originally published in April 1952.

The Roustabout Serenade

Long ago, a crew of happy-go-lucky laborers known as traveling roustabouts installed the first system of waterworks in Kingstree. Those powerful young men seemed to radiate good health. They worked long hours digging ditches and laying sewer pipes, installing a septic tank and erecting a storage tank for the town's reserve supply of water. It stood high in the air near the police station on Mill Street. Stationary steel ladders reached from the ground to a narrow platform around the tank, and there was a single guardrail around the platform. "Kingstree, S.C.," was painted in large white letters on the dark tank, which was not as big as the one now on the same spot.

The construction boss, who was a stern, heavy-set fellow, dismissed the roustabouts every Saturday at noon. They dressed in Sunday clothes and went out on the town—such as it was. And all immediately got high as Georgia pines. That did nothing to enhance their local reputations—about which they didn't give a hoot in a busy time of cussing, as a popular saying went.

But their antics did provide interesting conversation for the disapproving villagers whose daughters were not allowed to date such White Trash. It wasn't that the parents scorned the laborers. They respected honest toil, but coarse White Trash was their pet abomination.

When the young roustabouts first hit town, they made a play for the local girls just on chance, but as their work had taken them from village to village, they weren't surprised at their lack of success in Kingstree. Maybe they reasoned that they had nothing to lose, and at least it was fun to try.

One mid-afternoon, when the last coat of paint had been put on the sign on the water tank, the construction boss announced that the job was finished, and he went his weary way. The jubilant crew, still in work clothes, decided to pitch a farewell party before heading for the next job. Of all places to pitch a party, they chose that platform high in the air. They sent somebody for booze, and it wasn't long before all had scrambled up the ladders, and the celebrating began. Two played leapfrog around and around the platform, one pretended to skin the cat on the guardrail, while the others raised their voices in "Sweet Adeline."

The public took notice when the harmonizing became louder. An appreciative audience of men, women and children gathered on the ground as the roustabouts belted out "Who Threw the Overalls in Mrs. Murphy's Chowder?" It was followed by "The Railroad Rag" and "Goodby, my Lover, Goodby." On the second verse of "The Girl I Left Behind Me," the singers changed it to "The Girls We Left Behind Us," and they laughed uproariously. But they really went into high gear on "Dixie." When one stood on his hands with both feet waving like flags in the air, the audience clapped and cheered.

The lone policeman on duty in the peaceful village was stout and middle-aged and troubled with corns. He appeared on the scene and stared a moment in disbelief, then he shouted impatiently for the roustabouts to come down before they broke their fool necks. They shouted joyfully for him to come up and join the fun. They waved bottles invitingly. The audience on the ground loved it. The conscientious policeman threatened sternly to arrest the merrymakers for drunkenness and disturbing the peace. The merrymakers threatened happily to sue the policeman for false arrest above the town limits. The audience howled with delight.

The policeman preserved his dignity by leaving to consult the mayor on that point of law, and he never came back. Mayor L. Percy Kinder was too wise to let the dutiful policeman climb to the top of a high ladder with the chance of getting conked on the head with a bottle when he got there. Possibly the mayor felt sympathetic toward the merrymakers, as he himself had been a gay, young sport who flew high before time and a bay window grounded him forever.

Besides, the roustabouts had made it possible for the mayor to enjoy the luxury of stretching out in a full-length bathtub. Before they installed the waterworks, His Honor, the mayor, had to coil himself like a pile of wet wash in a round, tin tub by the kitchen stove while small children peeped through cracks to see the free show.

Anyway, the jolly roustabouts cavorted until they were in the mood to leave town. Nobody got hurt, nobody got arrested, nobody got sued and nobody got conked. With time, even the good-natured policeman enjoyed telling how those happy young bucks had managed to out-fox him.

Material from columns originally published in October 1971.

Potter's Raiders

Not long ago, some young people astonished me by saying they had never heard of Potter's Raid in Williamsburg County. However, it's easy to understand their lack of information on the subject when you realize that histories of South Carolina written in recent years make little or no mention of that once-famous raid, the immediate objective of which was to burn Kingstree as Sherman's army had burned Columbia a few weeks earlier in the year 1865.

But the War Between the States wasn't history to us. It was too near. We knew Confederate veterans personally. We could name men killed in battle, for we knew relatives who still grieved for them. And we knew a white-haired old lady, Miss Bette McClary, who would remain forever true to the handsome young lover who had asked her to wait for him. I still remember the bitterness in her voice as she said, "The Damn-Yankees killed the only man I ever loved." That wasn't an oath then. "Damn-Yankee" was one word, and ladies who would not have been guilty of using such a coarse expression as "dog-gone" used it with impunity.

When President Lincoln was assassinated a week after Lee's surrender, Williamsburg District, like the rest of the despairing South, lost hope of any fair consideration. With weaker and more vindictive men at the helm in Washington, ruffians from both the North and South would continue to overrun the country. Already, Georgetown, South Carolina, had been burned and pillaged by General Potter's Raiders, who were composed of power-mad Union soldiers and camp followers, and had been joined by roving bands of southern robbers and other renegades, totaling several thousand men.

It was evidently Potter's ambition to imitate Sherman's notorious march to the sea. It had been over two years since President Lincoln issued the Emancipation Proclamation, but vast numbers of Negro slaves in Williamsburg had chosen to remain on the plantations they called home, and 'til this day, many of their descendants are still living in the self-same communities. However, hundreds of the younger Colored men had believed the wild tales going the rounds that the Yankees would accept them as equals and give them everything they needed, so they slipped away by night to join Potter's Raiders in Georgetown District. In their excitement, those Negroes lost sight of the fact that their own wives, children, sisters and aged parents, whom they were deserting, would suffer the same fate as white people at the hands of the approaching thieves, rapists, and murderers.

When Potter's Raiders decided to leave the smoldering ruins in Georgetown and head for Williamsburg, there was neither telegraph nor telephone by which warning could be sent ahead, but couriers traveled in relays to spread the tidings along the route. When the terrifying message, "The Yankees are coming!" was received at one farm, another courier was sent to carry it on to the next, then on and on, chain fashion, all over the district. From Williamsburg, the warning was fanned out over adjoining districts. Families everywhere were in the grip of helpless terror for many able-bodied men who had not been killed or wounded in battle were still many miles away. The strain of waiting was almost unbearable.

In the meantime, the Raiders were making a leisurely march toward Kingstree, striking camp when and where it pleased their fancy, different bands branching out to shower misery and destruction upon homes in ever-widening circles. As farm after farm was laid waste, the news traveled ahead that few homes had been left standing in the section south of Black River. The Raiders were often half-drunk on barrels of whiskey, rum and wine stolen along their route and had become like frenzied savages bent upon destroying everything in sight, even cutting down fruit trees, grapevines and fine shade trees prized by plantation owners. They took horses and mules for their own use but wantonly slaughtered all the oxen, cows, hogs and dogs, as well as all fowl, within range of their guns or swords and left the carcasses to rot where they fell.

Maddened by mob-hysteria, the Raiders smashed jars of fruit and vegetables, as well as empty jars saved for future use. Fresh vegetables growing in gardens were deliberately trampled or cut down. It was like a game for the Raiders to mix flour, rice, meal, sugar and salt with manure in the horse lots. Potato bags were torn open, and kerosene poured into them before the torch was applied; bales of cotton were ruined in like manner. Haystacks, corn barns and smokehouses for cured meats were burned to the ground.

Though the location of buried jewelry and other valuables was pointed out to the Raiders by an occasional treacherous Negro, more often it was at the point of a gun or a sword that a slave betrayed his White folks. Women and children of both races who had hidden together in the swamps were searched out by Potter's men and brought back to witness the destruction of their own homes. There were many other crimes too horrible to be described here.

An occasional home was left standing when Potter himself headed one of the smaller marauding bands. Such was the case when the Raiders reached the old Boyd home about a quarter-mile off the Kingstree-Andrews Highway. After watching his men rush into their usual orgy of destruction, Potter dismounted from his horse and indulged his own sadistic pleasure by gruffly ordering the Boyd's terrified little daughter—Mary Agnes, who was only eight years old—to hold his horse. For the moment, the child's hatred of Potter overshadowed her terror. "I'll do no such thing!" she flared defiantly, but her mother, fearing worse might be in store for her child, firmly commanded her to obey the general.

Fortunately, perhaps, the little girl offered no further resistance and numbly stood there holding Potter's horse while his men destroyed her family's livestock and provisions, even the eggs on which the hens were sitting. Feather pillows and mattresses were slashed open, and a large morocco-bound Bible that the family had treasured was deliberately mutilated.

The plantation carpenter, who had previously stood faithfully by his White folks, caught the contagious madness. Earlier, he had been trusted to hide the family's silverware and had made an opening in a wall, deposited the silver inside, then repaired the wall so skillfully the alteration could not be detected.

Swept by the frenzied excitement of the Raiders, the Negro dashed to the hiding place and ripped it open and with his arms full of fine old silver, which had been cherished for generations, he gleefully shouted to the other fiends, "This is mine now!" It would be interesting to know whether the general, at that moment, was reminded of another traitor and his "thirty pieces of silver." When the Raiders left, the carpenter and the silver went with them.

It was from the Boyd home that a courier was sent with the dreaded message, "The Yankees are coming!"

Colonel James F. Pressley, who was at home recuperating from wounds received in the Battle of Atlanta, was placed in command of a force numbering about 1,600 and made up of old men, soldiers who had returned home, Negroes who had remained loyal and young boys in their early teens, including the late Dr. D.C. Scott, who was then only fifteen years old.

This force, which was all Williamsburg District could muster against the thousands under Potter's command, was deployed at strategic points up and

A reunion of Confederate Veterans in Kingstree early in the twentieth century. *Photograph courtesy of Williamsburgh Historical Museum.*

down the river. Colonel Pressley headed a band that reached Lower Bridge a few hours before the Raiders. Pressley's men tore up the wooden bridge and piled the material for quick burning, lest it fall into enemy hands, and as the Raiders approached the far bank, H.D. Shaw struck a match to the pile.

The Raiders immediately opened fire, and many volleys were exchanged. Fortunately for the Williamsburg men, the river was very high, and it was impossible for the Raiders to build a bridge or cross the river under fire from Pressley's band. That night, Captain John E. Scott swam across the swollen stream under cover of darkness and scuttled a number of small boats he knew to be tied on the far side.

Next day, as the Raiders moved westward along the river, Pressley's forces moved likewise. When Potter reached Kingstree, he found another burned bridge, and all other bridges up and down the river were likewise torn up or burned. Everywhere Potter's men attempted to cross the stream, they were met with gunfire.

It's likely that Potter, with his vast superiority in strength, could have taken this section eventually, had he been so minded, but his hordes evidently had more relish for ravaging helpless plantations than facing withering gunfire, so they finally decided to bypass Kingstree and wend their leisurely way onward.

It wasn't long before dissention arose among Potter's own forces, which had been augmented by ever-increasing numbers of Negroes. Though there had been many slaves in the North, they had been owned mostly by wealthy people who could afford staffs of domestic servants, for there were no money-making cotton fields as in the South. Therefore, many of Potter's Raiders had never seen a Colored person before the War. Trouble arose between the two races. A number of Williamsburg Negroes deserted the Raiders, and by hiding in the daytime and traveling at night, they finally made their half-starved way back home. But the Boyd's carpenter with his prized silverware was never heard from again.

Material from columns originally published in March 1952.

Our Confederate Yankee

A few weeks ago, there was something in the news about a little town with enough sense of humor to celebrate Sucker Day, lest it forget the time a smooth-talking stranger collected money in advance for a circus that never showed up. If Kingstree ever decided to name a Sucker Day, we might do well to consider the tenth of May in memory of a crazy thing that happened here in 1910.

Though it had been more than forty years since General Robert E. Lee surrendered to General Ulysses S. Grant, loyalty to the fallen Confederacy was still very much alive in Williamsburg County. For some time, it had been the dream of the local United Daughters of the Confederacy chapter to erect a Confederate monument, and members had worked long and diligently toward that end. Public sentiment was with them, but cash contributions were few and far between, as those were the days when money was still scarce as the proverbial hen's teeth. But the ladies persevered with a determination the like of which is seldom seen in this era of quick money.

In winter they held many public hot suppers, and in summer they held ice cream socials and strawberry festivals. At last, the UDC members saw their goal in sight, and they placed an order for a handsome granite monument, bearing a fitting inscription composed by Charles W. Wolfe, owner and editor of the *County Record*. An Italian sculptor of high repute was commissioned to carve the figure of a Confederate soldier to stand on top of the tall shaft as a lasting symbol of the honor and reverence in which all Confederate fighting men would be held forevermore.

When the heavy pieces arrived by freight, the villagers enjoyed watching the workmen erect the monument at the intersection of Main and Academy Streets, but all such activity was only a buildup to the big day when the

Downtown Kingstree was crowded with people on May 10, 1910, for the official unveiling of the monument. *Photograph courtesy of W.E. Jenkinson III.*

figure of the soldier would be unveiled. The tenth of May was chosen as the most appropriate date for the proud ceremony.

Early that morning, people from all over the county began arriving in buggies, wagons, road carts and carriages. There was also a sprinkling of automobiles with bodies built high off the ground to miss stumps in the roads. Children carrying flowers met at the grammar school for the annual Memorial Day parade through the streets. Confederate veterans who were honored each year with a sumptuous midday banquet following the traditional exercises arrived early.

Though all those veterans were heroes, a few were men first and heroes second. They knew that the law required the county dispensary—forerunner of the modern package shops—to remain closed on holidays, so it was their custom to grapevine the word to some friend in town to look out for them. Dr. W.G. Gamble's drugstore was on Main Street, and his clerk, Isaiah Tisdale, affectionately known as "Doctor" Tisdale, was a fellow whose friends could depend on him. Several of the veterans who had traveled many miles over rough roads lost little time before casually dropping by the drugstore.

There they hung around, though there wasn't any soda fountain, 'til no ladies were in sight, then looked under the counter for their bottles or jugs of what they chose to call "the milk of human kindness." Now, men have

C.W. Wolfe in his Citadel uniform in 1889. *Photograph courtesy of Williamsburgh Historical Museum.*

The monument stood in the intersection of Main and Academy streets until the late 1950s. *Photograph courtesy of Williamsburgh Historical Museum.*

The crowd attending the dedication of the monument poses in front of the base. *Photograph courtesy of Williamsburgh Historical Museum.*

been trying since time began (without too much success, I might add) to keep their secrets from women. But then, as now, those jugs and bottles were no secret. And by some strange means better left unexplained, a little ipecac had found its way into each one.

At first the thirsty heroes took only gentlemenly drinks, just enough to put them into the proper mellow mood to enjoy the impassioned speeches that were the order of the day, and they detected nothing amiss. They joined the throng on the corner in time for the unveiling proper. Finally, the great moment arrived, and all eyes were lifted eagerly for the first breathless glimpse of the noble figure in the hallowed Confederate uniform. But do you know what was on top of our Confederate monument? A Yankee!

The Italian sculptor had made a mistake. And that's what I call a masterpiece of understatement. He knew that the Rebels and Yankees who had fought each other in the War Between the States were all Americans but didn't know there was any difference in their uniforms. Can you beat that?

One veteran, who had brought his liquid refreshments from home and consequently had a head start on the others, took one look at the Yankee, then was seen to stagger to the grass on the courthouse square where he held up both hands and cried out in a loud voice, "Grant, I surrender!" Then he pitched forward on his face. Others, in a state of shock, hurried back to the drugstore. Each felt the need of a quick bracer—and a big one—then another. But suddenly, all felt the pressing need for fresh air or something. They managed to reach the back premises of the courthouse square before the ipecac hit them full force. But it's best to draw a curtain on the rest of that scene.

Material from columns originally published in April 1952.

Part II
Village School

Going to School

I was crazy to get big enough to go to school. Not that I was troubled by any burning thirst for knowledge, but I had a deep yearning for a lunch pail like the one Mary carried. That cute little tin bucket with tight-fitting lid was bright as silver and would be a collector's item today.

Children walked the unpaved miles to and from the one-room schoolhouse that was in the woods below the farms, now owned by Mary Agnes Brown, Peden Coward and Henry Shaw. Finally, it was decided to let me begin school if I could hold out to walk without bothering the larger children to tote me. There was no age requirement as to beginners, nor any objections to starting or stopping in the middle of the term.

My joy knew no bounds—'til I saw Mother fixing lunch for Mary and me in the same bucket, a common kitchen bucket at that. I set up a wail. I wanted a little bucket of my own, as if a magic wand could produce one. Mary set up a wail because she didn't want to carry a kitchen bucket. But carry it she did, and we both left home mad.

Other children appeared from side roads and joined Mary and me. Nobody hurried. Our group paused to examine a delicate trail left by a big snake that had crossed the road for no apparent reason other than to get to the other side. We speculated on the fate of a small, brown rabbit, darting across the road to vanish in a ditch full of briars. We stopped to gather some of the ripe seeds from a patch of dusty teaweeds and sat down in the sand to eat them. The group stopped again to investigate a dead frog stuck on the long thorn of a wild plum bush. The older children discussed a nearby farmer's vicious bull that sometimes jumped the fence and went on rampages. The tales that grew with the telling about Mr. Todd's white-face cow (as they called the bull) were as familiar as the nursery rhyme about the cow jumping over the moon.

We eyed every clump of bushes we came to lest Mr. Todd's white-face cow be hiding there. That cow had horns a yard long, the boys declared, and he would stick his horns through you and toss you high into the air just for fun. When you fell back to the ground, he would jump on you with all four feet and stomp you to mush. Then he would eat your gizzard. Mr. Todd's white-face cow liked gizzards better than candy or cake.

Finally we neared the unpainted, but picturesque, wooden schoolhouse that time had bleached a silver gray. It nestled between two live oaks, which were probably a hundred years old, their giant limbs spreading fifteen or more feet in all directions.

At the schoolhouse, we drank our fill of cool water bubbling from a spring and then joined the games. Playing outdoors, I thought school wonderful. But then the loud clang of a brass handbell called us inside, and my disillusionment began. The large, unpainted room—in which pupils of all ages were taught by one schoolmaster—was drab and dreary and had no desks. Pupils sat on benches without backs around three walls that had never been ceiled. My feet couldn't touch the floor. A homemade table at the far end of the oblong room served as the teacher's desk, but he did have a chair with a back.

I think his name was Purvis Nelson. He was tall and big-boned and he had a heavy moustache and thick eyebrows. A bunch of long switches leaned against the wall behind him, but I didn't know they were used only on boys. When Mr. Nelson drew his brows together and eyed me, I couldn't have been more terrified had he been a grizzly bear.

At the long recess we ate lunch and bent small saplings down to be ridden as horses, with the thrilling risk of being catapulted skyward should the saplings prove strong enough to spring back to their original upright positions. We played drop the handkerchief and drank water from a nearby branch.

At recess, I whispered to my sister Mary, who was three years older than I, that I was going home. She whispered back fearfully, "You can't go by yourself. Mr. Todd's white-face cow might stomp you to mush and eat your gizzard." So I went back into the schoolhouse to suffer some more.

The teacher put the other children to drawing circles, squares and triangles on their slates. Then he took a seat behind his desk, tilted his chair back, put his big feet on top of the desk and went to sleep. Whereupon the children began drawing everything except circles, squares and triangles, but smothered their giggles having no desire to wake the teacher before time to go home.

Asleep on the job, the teacher was out of his misery for the time being, but I was still in mine. I couldn't even enjoy the other children's smothered giggles when a big flock of turkeys from a nearby farm paused to graze close to the schoolhouse. Naturally stupid, the turkeys stood still with necks stretched high every time a teenaged boy whispered, "Shoo!" through an open knothole in the wall behind his bench. Then the gobblers gobbled loudly, and the hens chirped shrill alarms time after time without moving 'til the children were nearly strangling, though all were used to the dumb ways of turkeys.

I couldn't take my eyes off the sleeping giant. All of a sudden he gave a convulsive jerk, and his heavy snore ripped through the room like the roar of a wild beast. I bolted out the door, and the turkeys rose with the ease of buzzards to light in the tops of the tallest pines. Up the road I went, headed for home and Mother, fast as I could make it in the sand, expecting to hear the teacher with his switches coming behind me any minute.

I tried to stop crying, the better to watch the thick woods bordering the road, and from which Mr. Todd's white-faced cow was sure to spring. Presently, I heard the pounding of heavy hoofbeats coming fast behind me, and I knew it was the cow. I was too scared to look back and too tired to run faster. I tripped on something and fell, and before I could get up, I heard my name called and I recognized Papa's voice. He was on horseback. When he picked me up and got back into the saddle, holding me close, neither of us said anything. "Papa," I finally sobbed when I could get my breath, "will I have to go back to school tomorrow?"

He leaned down to kiss my head and said, "No, Baby!" My world was right again, and I went to sleep in his arms.

Material from columns originally published in January 1952, May 1971 and June 1971.

School Days

Academy Street was named for the Williamsburg Academy, a private school that flourished at the head of that street during the Reconstruction period following the Civil War. However, the first school that I attended was Kingstree Academy, where the Carnegie Library now stands on the corner of Hampton Avenue and Mill Street. It was a sprawling one-story frame structure painted white with a bell tower on top. Some of the spacious rooms held two small grades taught by one teacher. A large first grade was taught in a nearby cottage on Mill Street. That cottage is now owned by Mrs. Edwina Smeltzer and faces the three-story brick hardware store recently built by J.B. Alsbrook.

I never took first grade anywhere. In those casual times, children could enroll in any grade they pleased. Though I had previously attended school only one day in my life, it pleased me—or rather my sister, Mary—to enroll me in the second grade at the academy. I don't know where Mother was that day. Mary, who was nearly three years older than I, had already taught me to spell "cat" and "rat," and she was very ambitious for her little sister. She herself had taken to schooling like the proverbial duck to water, but to me a schoolhouse was a jail. I wanted out—to be free to play with my dolls, to skip rope, to fish with wild onion stems in tiny doodlebug holes in the yard, or to climb a tree and sit on a limb, doing nothing, just enjoying the world. There was no place in my world for education.

My teacher was Miss Nina Riser of Newberry. She had a hard time teaching me to spell "cylinder," and I'm still wondering what that long word was doing in a second-grade speller. By some miracle I managed to get through the grade in one year, but I had to take a later grade twice. I don't remember which, but I do remember hiding under the bed to cry because I had failed my exams. I was certain I had disgraced our family forever

The Williamsburg Academy, which stood at the head of Academy Street. *Photograph courtesy of Williamsburgh Historical Museum.*

The Kingstree Academy on the corner of Mill Street and Hampton Avenue. *Photograph courtesy of Williamsburgh Historical Museum.*

until Mother and Mary explained that it was better to take the grade over, and then school would be easier for me. And so it proved, for I never again flunked an examination.

The late Mr. W.W. Boddie was superintendent of the academy, and the next in command was the principal, Mr. Ernest Wiggins. The other teachers were women. Years later, Mr. Boddie wrote *Boddie's History of Williamsburg County*, a large, thick volume, handsomely bound and containing a wealth of information, which would have been lost to posterity had he not undertaken the monumental task of compiling the data. Other children at the academy whispered to me that Mr. Boddie was in love with Helen Scott, who was one of the seniors and was the only daughter of Dr. and Mrs. D.C. Scott. Their gossip must have been true, as Mr. Boddie and Helen did marry after she finished college.

Material from columns originally published in May 1970.

Recess

Long before the days of playground equipment and supervised games, children created their own diversions at recess in the large cleared areas around the schools. At Kingstree Academy, one of the most popular games was a fiendish thing called whiplash. About a dozen children standing in a row joined hands, the tallest at the head and on down the line, with the smallest at the tag end. Then the tallest, who was the head of the whip, led off at a fast run, the others stringing out in a line behind him like a trailing whip. When all got going at a good clip, the leader suddenly swerved, which caused the whip to "lash." Invariably, the child at the tag end lost his grip and was sent spinning heels over head, wherein lay the fun for the other demons.

At recess my first day in school, such a line was forming, headed by Marion Gilland and Adelaide Harper—both tall, lanky children. Somebody asked if I wanted to play. I did, so they kindly let me be the tag end. About the next thing I knew, I was turning somersaults in one direction while the lunch I had been eating was turning in another. When I stopped rolling and began howling, Marion and Adelaide ran to comfort me. While Marion brushed the sand off me, Adelaide brushed the sand off my big buttermilk biscuit and sausage with the hem of her skirt. So pretty soon things were again all right with me, as I didn't mind a little grit in my food.

Dr. and Mrs. Jack Brockington lived on Hampton Avenue next door to the Academy. Their only child, Ada, was the envy of the other small fry. There was a high fence of wide vertical boards between the Brockington back premises and the play area around the Academy. Children were forbidden to leave the grounds for any reason short of death or disaster, but at recess little Ada would pick her chance. Then she would shimmy to

Marion Gilland O'Bryan years after she attended Kingstree Academy. *Photograph courtesy of Williamsburgh Historical Museum.*

the top of the fence with the ease of a cat squirrel, jump to the ground on the other side, dart into the kitchen at home, gobble something to eat, dart out with greasy mouth, and still chewing, be back over the fence before she was missed.

Material from columns originally published in May 1970.

Crowning Silas Stutts

Long ago, a boy named Silas Stutts was in grammar school at Kingstree Academy. He was a slim chap with a thick shock of tawny hair and sat behind his sweetheart Gertrude Oliver, a pretty child whose brown hair hung in a plait down her back. At times Silas dipped the plait into a stationary inkwell on his desk as one way to get her attention. I sat behind Silas.

Silas was late the day we got our first geographies, which were wide, thin books with hard covers. When Silas finally slipped into his place, I was looking at a colored map in my new book and paid no attention to him. Then I glanced up and saw that his head had been shaved clean. I stared a moment in stunned revulsion at that naked skull, then impulsively shut my book, lifted it with both hands as high as I could and brought it down with all my strength on his head.

The pop sounded like a pistol shot in the quiet room. Silas yelped and sprang up. The teacher e-e-eek-ed and rose up. I cringed and shrank down, waiting for doom to strike. It did.

Miss Bertha Wells gave me ten demerits, the limit for a child to receive in one month without getting a switching in the principal's office. Many boys got switched, but I don't recall that a girl ever did.

Miss Wells also made me stay in without lunch at recess for a week. She said that was because of my stubbornness in refusing to tell why I did such an unladylike thing. Silas kept urging me to say that he had pinched me, but I wouldn't, so he daily slipped me half his lunch to gobble at recess during the few minutes the teacher was out of the room. Each time she returned she asked if I wanted to tell her why I had misbehaved, and I meekly answered, "No, ma'am." How could I tell her? To this day I don't know why I crowned Silas.

It wasn't my piety that kept me from pretending that Silas had pinched me. It was instinctive self-preservation. A vendetta by other small fry could be worse than any teacher's punishment. Children learned early not to tattle. It was all right to kick and scream if in trouble, but it was a sin to whimper and tell how you got there—that is, if somebody else might get a switching in the deal. A tattler was given the cruel, cold-shoulder treatment indefinitely.

Material from columns originally published in June 1970.

Picker

L ong ago there was a perfect little devil called Picker in grammar school at Kingstree Academy. Other pupils adored him, but his teachers longed to kill him.

I have forgotten why the boy was called Picker, but he was a born comedian and could convulse half a schoolroom just by lifting an eyebrow at the right moment, then appear innocent as an angel by the time a teacher could glance his way. He had been made to stand in the corner, had been kept in at recess and after school, and had been switched so often for getting too many demerits in one month that he didn't count any of them as punishment. Nothing had put a damper on his gay spirits.

Though Picker always began the day clean, he looked like a tramp before it was over, which was all right with him—just so he didn't look sissy. He was a well-built youngster with a straight back and shoulders so erect that he had a military bearing.

We had never heard of a puppet show, but Picker could do things with his ever-present handkerchief that would have done credit to an expert. One balmy spring day, Picker began playing with his handkerchief, which, as usual, was held in the aisle where the teacher couldn't see it.

He whispered, "Look," to Tommie Gilland, who sat behind him, and who, also as usual, was staring with longing out one of the big windows in the wall by their desks.

I sat behind Tommie, and when he whispered to me, "Watch Picker," I knew to pass the word. The whole row was watching as Picker rolled the opposite edges of his handkerchief toward each other, looped it, then pulled the four corners through the loop. After a little, he whispered, "Big fat bullfrog." Instantly, the thing became a live frog with long hind legs kicking comically, and our suppressed laughter burst out.

The teacher knew that Picker was at the root of the disturbance but also knew that she couldn't prove it, so she pretended ignorance. No sooner had she quieted the room than Picker again began playing with his handkerchief while we watched. Presently, he whispered, "Old dead goose." With the head grasped in Picker's fist, the long neck was stretched 'til it was a sight, the wings and legs hanging limp in death. It saddened us. Then Picker worked more magic. When the tail began to twitch briskly from side to side, we clamped our hands over our mouths.

A goose with romance on his mind was nothing new to us who saw flocks of geese daily. A warning twitch of a goose's tail, and he would take off as fast as his long legs would carry him toward the female of his choice. She instantly took off in the opposite direction as fast as her short legs could carry her, just for the fun of the chase, as the outcome was a foregone conclusion.

Picker made his goose's legs begin running at full speed, and one child sputtered. The rest of us exploded. That was the last straw for the teacher. She didn't ask any questions, knowing that nobody would tell her anyway. Besides, who would believe a child who said that the handkerchief into which Picker was innocently blowing his nose was a big live bullfrog or an old dead goose come to life in a big way?

The teacher stomped to where Picker sat, grabbed him by the ear, lifted him almost bodily from the seat, marched him to the outside door and all but threw him down the steps, with orders not to return until called. When she went back to her desk and busied herself there, the silence in the room was thick with resentment. It had done something to us to see her shame our hero and for him to go down without a fight. But we should have known Picker better.

Presently, Tommie, who had been staring sadly out the window, whispered excitedly to me, "Pass the word." All who could looked out a window. There was Picker in the bright sunlight a few yards away. But do you think he was crying or downcast? No, indeed.

He had shed his pants and had turned his naked backside squarely up to the schoolhouse. His head was bowed, but it was between his knees, and his tongue was stuck out as far as it would go, the better to show just what he thought of schools and education.

Never on land or sea has there been a more eloquent gesture, and never again in my life have I seen anything so white as Picker's naked skin that day. I'm sorry I don't remember what punishment poor little Picker got. At least they didn't kill him.

Material from columns originally published in June 1970.

Busting China Thunder-Jugs

The first big school in Williamsburg County was on the northeast corner of Brooks and School Streets in Kingstree. It was a two-story, red brick building with a bell tower on top and was called Kingstree Graded and High School. The wooden academy on the corner of Hampton Avenue and Mill Street, where I began school, had been closed, and all pupils transferred to the new building.

There was a sturdy, four-foot iron fence around the grounds, and no pupil could go outside without permission, much less climb over the fence.

To be caught with a slingshot meant a sure switching by the superintendent, but every little boy in grammar school knew places to hide them when not in use.

There was no indoor plumbing then, and in private homes, each bedroom had a wooden washstand on which stood a large china pitcher and basin. The white china had gay flowers painted on it—big pink or red roses or geraniums or bright morning glories, all with bright green leaves. A matching chamber pot was kept under the bed.

A strip of farm land lay between School Street, which was then only a narrow dirt road, and the Atlantic Coast Line Railroad. The lone one-story frame house on the strip had front and back porches. It belonged to Dr. Harry Brown, a Negro root doctor who practiced witchcraft when the moon was right and also did a little preaching and farming on the side. There was a perpetual feud between Dr. Brown and the boys in grammar school, but every skirmish seemed to end in a draw.

Dr. Brown's chamber pot had red roses on it, and one scorching hot morning, he put it out to sun near his back steps. Unfortunately, Dr. Brown's house was within sling-shot range of the little boys inside the iron fence. At recess Dr. Brown went to Superintendent Bethea, who was strolling in the

The Kingstree Graded and High School was located on the corner of Brooks and School streets. *Photograph courtesy of Williamsburgh Historical Museum.*

shade under a spreading oak tree. "Professor," said Dr. Brown with great dignity, "I want to report that Picker Funk busted my china thunder-jug with his slingshot."

Picker, who was a very resourceful lad, declared with equal dignity that the hot sun must have busted the doctor's pot, only he called it a compound word that won't bear repeating here. But poor Picker still had the slingshot on his hip, and one of his pockets was full of pebbles. Picker got a switching, but that was nothing new to him. Mischievous Picker had learned to take a switching in his stride, and he went his usual way undaunted.

That night, the wooden privy behind Dr. Brown's house got turned over backwards, but nobody was able to prove that Picker, with the help of his loyal buddies, had done the dastardly deed. So that skirmish also ended in a draw.

Strangely enough, Dr. Brown and the little boys really liked each other, and all enjoyed the excitement of their seesaw war of wits.

Part III
Village Characters

Otis Arrowsmith

In Kingstree long ago, our childhood hero was Otis Arrowsmith. Otis was never in too big a hurry to pause a few moments as he walked (no cars then) by a yard where children at play had run to the picket fence to greet him.

He would delight us with miraculous tales that made "The Three Bears" seem like tame rabbits. I'm sure a collection of those stories that Otis made up as he told them would have become a bestseller.

A few pompous souls, including some of his older relatives, told Otis he was "the biggest liar unhung." They predicted that he would never "amount to a tinker's damn" with his lazy, loose-jointed walk and his "Come-day, go-day, God-send-Sunday" (which meant extra-happy) disposition.

Was Otis insulted? Not in the least. With a chuckle in his deep bass voice, he told the prophets of doom that he himself would still be whistling "Dixie" long after they had worried themselves into their graves. And he was. Best of all, Otis continued to have a fine time living 'til the last breath left him.

Otis fooled them in many ways. In time, he married Miss Luna Tribble, who was one of my favorite teachers, and Otis was elected to the South Carolina legislature.

Otis's gift for storytelling really came into its own when silent movies first hit Kingstree. While the rest of the bewildered audience sat in darkness watching the silent actors cavorting on the screen, Otis kept up a constant stream of explanation to any child near him. No doubt his version was better than the original script, and it at least had the merit of giving the audience some glimmer of what the show was trying to tell them.

Once, when the screen suddenly went blank, a ghostly voice from the loft broke the dark silence, "One moment, please, while the operator changes the fil-lum."

A little boy with Otis piped out uneasily, "What's the matter?"

Otis scoffed, "Nothing, except that son-of-a-bee has broken the film again." And without lowering his voice, Otis added, "Boy, do you want to pee-pee?"

Material from columns originally published in March 1970.

The Old Lamplighter

Long ago, when I was a small child in Kingstree, there was no electricity. At street corners, the picturesque kerosene lamps mounted on sturdy posts about seven feet tall were lit at dusk and extinguished at dawn by a lamplighter in a high silk hat and black cutaway coat.

He looked like a character from a novel by Charles Dickens, then rated the world's most popular author. 'Til this day, I still think of our lamplighter every time I see a Christmas scene that includes an old English street lamp.

I could fill a book about Reverend Jimmy Harper, as our Colored lamplighter called himself. His wife, Frances, was a wonderful cook with a droll humor, but she had a quick temper, and she often yelled that Jimmy couldn't be a preacher because no Negro, including her, would believe anything he said, even with his hand on the Holy Bible. At this, Jimmy just chuckled and went his usual amiable way. Yet, he had such an engaging personality that everybody of both races liked him, and Frances adored him.

Everything Jimmy wanted, Jimmy got, but he had never been known to pay anybody for anything. He and his wife, children, grandchildren and assorted relatives lived in one house in the big backyard of Mr. and Mrs. T.M. Gilland Sr. The silk hat had once belonged to Mr. Gilland, and the cutaway coat had been bought on credit from Reverend Erasmus Ervin, the trusting pastor of our historic Presbyterian church.

Jimmy once put a classic fooling on a slick agent who was traveling through the wilds selling tombstones. With only a promise as a down payment, Jimmy placed an order for his own tombstone. Weeks later, when the agent came to make delivery, he couldn't find Jimmy, who had seen him first. Finally, the agent angrily unloaded the stone by Jimmy's doorsteps and said he would be back Saturday to collect. The children had a fine time running their fingers over the large chiseled letters: REV. JIMMY HARPER.

When the agent came Saturday, he couldn't find Jimmy or the tombstone. Both were hidden in the hayloft above the carriage house in the big horse lot.

After numerous trips in vain, the agent quit coming. Maybe the poor man had died, but Jimmy lived many more years. In time, the tombstone must have been forgotten. Long after Jimmy's death, the carriage house burned, and the stone came tumbling down. By that time I was grown and had children of my own, who also had adored Jimmy. When I saw his name on the battered fragments on the ground, tears stung my eyes and I breathed silent thanks that there was a higher power to pass final judgment on mortals. Reverend Jimmy Harper's virtues—including his unfailing kindness to three generations of little children and his gentlemanly manners to one and all—exceeded by far his flagrant shortcomings.

Material from columns originally published in November 1970.

Willie Chin

The only Chinaman in Williamsburg County then was named Chin, but many people called him Willie. The little man lived alone in his hand laundry near T.J. Pendergrass's store. Month after month, he labored with his steaming tubs and smoothing irons, which were heated on wood-burning stoves.

The front door stayed open all day. Though Chin could speak very little English, he had learned to count money accurately, but he kept no books, and he would not credit anybody.

One day when Frank Watts, a prosperous jeweler who had never married, went for his laundry, he told Chin that he had just realized that he didn't have a cent with him, but he would send the money right back.

Chin eyed him solemnly, then intoned in his high sing-song voice: "Four shirts all splitty, four drawers all splitty. No money, no gitty."

Mr. Watts stormed out in a rage, but when he had cooled off, he sent back for his laundry, and he never tired of telling the joke on himself. His friends composed some clever limericks about his laundry, but they don't bear repeating here.

Chin never seemed to mind when small boys paused at his open door and teased him before taking to their heels. Possibly their harmless fun was welcomed by the lonely man in a strange country. But one day a group paused and shouted: "Chin, Chin, Chinaman eats dead rats. He won't save any for the poor house cats!"

Quick as a wink, a hot iron came hurtling through the door and barely grazed one of the fleeing little demons. Nobody did anything about it, as everybody's sympathy was with Willie Chin. After that, little boys held Chin in great respect.

Among the men now living in Kingstree who once teased the Chinaman, three—James Benton, George Hammet and Billie Britton—are on our police force. None will admit remembering who got grazed by Chin's hot iron, but I am fairly certain it was one of those three.

Material from columns originally published in June 1971.

Helpful Harry

B efore the electric chair came into use, it was the law in South Carolina that anyone convicted of murder in the first degree was hanged behind the jail in the county seat of the county in which he had been tried by a jury. And so it was in Kingstree.

When the murderer was a Negro, the other Negroes here refused to let him be buried in their cemeteries, which they regarded as hallowed ground. Even his own relatives refused to accept the poor sinner's body.

So far as I know, this county never had a potter's field in which criminals or paupers could be buried, as the living took care of their own dead. However, it became an established custom for a rejected murderer to be buried at the county's expense.

That's when Dr. Harry Brown, the farmer and root doctor who did a little preaching on the side, came on the scene. He had connections at the courthouse, where he was popular with the elected officials. No doubt he would now be called a stool pigeon, but then he was only "Helpful Harry."

Dr. Brown got the contract to bury any sinner who had been denied a final resting place among his own people. The county bought the wooden coffin, and Dr. Brown guaranteed decent burial for a cash fee. The spot chosen for the private burial was up to Dr. Brown. He had no land except the narrow strip on which he lived between the schoolhouse and the railroad, but his wife, Lizzie, wasn't about to let him bury a corpse near their home.

After a hanging, Dr. Brown waited 'til dark, then hitched his old gray mare to his rickety wagon and went to the jail for the coffin. He hauled it out of town and picked his chances to plant it on somebody else's land, preferably in a plowed field where the digging was easier. His luck held until one summer night when he barely cleared the town limits before burying the coffin on Mr. John T. Nelson's large farm, on which many Negroes were living. When they discovered the fresh grave, it didn't take them long to figure who was in it, nor to see his ghost roaming in the gloaming. The whole plantation became demoralized, and all work suffered.

When Mr. Nelson, who lived in town, heard what had happened, he ordered Dr. Brown to get that coffin off his land without delay. Dr. Brown, who would cheerfully promise anybody anything, promised Mr. Nelson to oblige immediately, if not sooner. But Dr. Brown had already collected his fee and spent it. Besides, he was a procrastinator, and whenever possible, he put off 'til the week after next what should have been done the week before last. So the days continued to roll by, and the ghost continued to "haunt" the plantation.

In the meantime, some young men-about-town, who had become more and more amused at the comical situation, decided after a few social drinks that it would be a good idea to play a joke on their friend, Dr. Harry Brown, and at the same time do a favor for their friend, Mr. Johnnie Nelson. They themselves would dig up the coffin. That night they went to the barroom in the Coleman House, a sprawling wooden hotel on Main Street, to wait for midnight and also to fortify themselves with a few stiff drinks before tackling the gruesome task.

For years, Dr. Brown's wife, Lizzie, had been the chief cook at the Coleman House, where she did a fine job. The well-fortified young men-about-town, who left the barroom at midnight, knew there were no children at the home of their friend Dr. Brown. They also knew it was his habit to open his front door every morning at daylight to see whether small schoolboys had played any tricks during the night. The young men made their leisurely way to where they had hidden a wagon and some shovels in the woods. It didn't take them long to dig up the coffin and haul it to town. There, they silently stood it on end against Dr. Brown's front door so that it would pitch into the room when he opened the door at daylight.

But their joke backfired. They knew there were no children in Dr. Brown's house, but they had forgotten that Lizzie left home before daylight to cook breakfast at the Coleman House. So it was poor Lizzie who opened the door and just missed being flattened by the coffin. Needless to say, she cooked no breakfast that day. She was too busy tongue-lashing Dr. Brown.

Women all over town were horrified by the cruel joke. Most husbands, afraid of their own wives' tongues, pretended to be equally horrified, but privately they were laughing themselves half to death. Schoolboys turned cartwheels of delight at the joke on Dr. Brown and didn't care who knew it. Ministers in all churches delivered impassioned orations on the subject. They declared unto heaven that the pranksters should be arrested for disturbing the peace and should be punished severely for their sinful wickedness. But the big question before the public was "Who did it?"

At least half of the men in town, including Dr. Brown, had learned within a few hours who had done it, but none would spill the beans to the ladies or to their pastors. The men reasoned that it wasn't fitting to discuss such coarse matters with ladies and gentlemen of refinement, to whom earthy humor was revolting.

At first, Dr. Brown himself was too busy to waste time in speculation. Lizzie had immediately laid down her own law to him, and for once in his life, he got in a hurry. He hastened to hitch his gray mare to his wagon, get the coffin off Lizzie's porch and get himself out of range of her voice. He buried the coffin in a beautiful stretch of woods that was then north of Kelley Street and east of Third Avenue.

Of course, the excitement wore itself out with time, and things settled back into the same old routine. But it was much longer before superstitious folks, who had to go through those woods after dark, stopped hearing strange sounds. Some swore it was the poor sinner's corpse stirring around to see whether Dr. Harry Brown was coming to move him again.

Material from columns originally published in July 1971.

Ed Nexsen

Before we moved to Kingstree, we lived on a farm. By the Kingstree-Andrews paved road, it is only two miles from town, but in the good old days, it was a long three miles through heavy sand beds and deep mud holes.

One hot summer day when my sister Mary and I were small, we were playing in the middle of the dirt road in front of the farmhouse. It had rained during the night, and we were packing the damp, white sand over our bare feet to make toad houses, which we firmly believed would be occupied by grateful frogs. Indeed, we had occasionally seen a small frog hiding in such a retreat, which set us to squealing with delight.

As there was practically no traffic in those leisurely times, we didn't bother to move when we saw a heavy wagon coming. We knew it would go around us. We recognized the matched pair of dappled gray mules from a farm some miles below ours, but we didn't recognize the young Negro driving them. Over six feet tall and powerfully built, he was standing with his bare feet slightly apart in the empty wagon, both hands in his pockets, the reins looped carelessly over his neck. As he swayed in easy rhythm with the motion of the wagon, his healthy black skin glistened like jet in the bright sunlight.

The wagon pulled to the side of the road and stopped. As the driver leaped to the ground, his teeth flashing in a happy smile, he said Mary and I had grown to be big girls while he was working in the turpentine woods in Florida. His name was Ed Nexsen, and many local people remembered him years later, when he was living in Kingstree, as the elderly giant who was given to patrolling the streets and back lots at all hours of the day or night, frequently talking to himself and declaring he was on the city police force.

But that day, he admired our toad houses and helped us to stick small flowers and twigs in their yards. Then he made another row of houses over his own huge feet, and to us they looked like mansions.

The local stores sold oranges only at Christmas, but Ed said that in Florida they grew on trees and were free for the picking. He told us of revival meetings and the glories of heaven above with its streets of pure gold, flowing with milk and honey. I had never seen any gold, except a few coins and some jewelry, which I wasn't allowed to play with, so I cared nothing for gold, and I couldn't stand honey, much less mixed with milk, of which we always had an abundance.

Most likely Ed had always been a mental case, for the condition grew worse rapidly. It had been rumored that he killed a man about a woman and left Florida only one jump ahead of the sheriff. He kept planning to go back for some wages due him, but he never did, and with time, he imagined there was a vast fortune waiting there for him. He talked about it the rest of his long life.

Looking back, it seems strange to me now that our paths continued to cross. After I grew up and was living with my own family on the same farm where Ed had made the toad houses, he reappeared from time to time. He had forgotten my name and called me Missy, but he remembered the toad houses, and he would sit under a tree in the grove and tell my son—Jack, who was then about eleven years old—marvelous tales about my childhood, and that he was going to give me a thousand dollars when he got his money from Florida, because we were blood kin.

It had been years since Ed did any regular work or slept in a bed. He roamed happily through the fields and woods between Kingstree and Salters, talking to himself about Florida and heaven, and always carrying a length of iron pipe on one shoulder, with a filthy burlap bag swinging by a strap from the other.

He appeared to stay in perfect health. Of course, I gave him food, but I never saw him eat any. He stuffed it and any money given him into the bulging sack with what he called "the key." He told Jack that he could work magic with the key to keep himself from harm and could "work root" with it, too. To me, he would admit only, "Missy, I got the key," but he would show Jack the little cloth tobacco sacks of dried snakes' skin, rabbit feet, owl claws, chopped eagle feathers and also small bottles of liquids, thickened with powder scraped from the horns of bulls.

My husband, John, was a favorite of Ed's. John had told Jack, and Roscoe Holloman who was our yardman, to keep an eye on Ed all the time he was on our premises, lest he prank with the artesian well from which water was piped to the house and barnyard. Sometimes he would stop at farms and tinker with the old-fashioned pitcher-pumps and make them produce better flows of water. At other times, Ed, who had tremendous strength, would pull a farmer's only pump out of the ground and leave it lying there.

Some years later, Ed began sleeping in back lots in the business district in Kingstree. He gradually attached himself to Police Chief George B. Hammet, who was kind to him, and pretty soon, Ed imagined that he himself was on the police force. Still carrying the iron pipe and burlap bag, he patrolled the back lots day and night, and not only kept order there, but threatened loafers who scattered litter. He claimed to be blood kin to Chief Hammet and his blonde wife, Gaynelle, and to the Hammet children who adored him as Jack had done earlier.

It was a little later that disaster struck. One day at the local bus station, Ed became enraged by something another Negro said to him (I've never known what it was) and Ed swung the iron pipe with all his might and crushed the man's skull. At long last, Ed Nexsen was committed to the Asylum for the Insane, where perhaps he should have been all the time.

Of course, the authorities there had trouble with Ed, who was like a wild beast put in a cage. John was then in the South Carolina Senate, and he and Chief Hammet went to the asylum to see about Ed. The authorities agreed to try letting Ed, who was by then an old man, have the run of the vast grounds, carrying a burlap sack to pick up trash and with a stick broom on his other shoulder. The plan worked well, and old Ed was soon happy again, rambling at will and talking to himself about Florida and heaven. Later he was allowed to come back to his beloved Kingstree, and eventually he died at the home of relatives.

Ed's faith that he would someday see his blessed Lord face to face never wavered. Who else except the Lord Almighty could have made a fair judgment of the sins and virtues of a human being such as Ed Nexsen had been?

A Dog Named Tham

Emil Arrowsmith liked to tell that when Flinn Gilland was five years old, he really looked like an angel with his fair skin and golden ringlets, and he still had a baby lisp in his speech. Early one morning, Flinn's mother sent him to the butcher shop to get a soup bone. On the way home, Flinn had the bright idea to let his big, shaggy dog named Sam carry the package in his mouth. The dog was used to carrying newspapers, but when he got a whiff of that bone, he grabbed the package and took off joyfully for parts unknown. Flinn ambled along in the same direction and came to M.F. Heller's Livery and Sales Stables, where Emil and some boon companions were loafing in straight chairs on the sidewalk. Flinn paused and lisped, "Hath anybody theen a dog named Tham with a thoup bone in hith mouth?"

Emil vows that the morning sunlight on Flinn's golden head formed a halo, the sight of which so unnerved Emil and his companions that they couldn't resume their discussion of beautiful women and fast horses or vice versa. They uneasily changed the subject to the current price of oats and hay. But they did give Flinn a dime to get another soup bone.

Flinn, did you ever find your bone? And do you remember when you first became interested in girls and wanted to put some "slick-um" on your hair but had none? When your mother next looked into her lard bucket and discovered dirty paw marks, you reluctantly admitted they were yours. When she found a straight, black hair and a straight, light hair also in her lard, you had to confess that Calhoun Dove and Carlyle Epps were your partners in crime.

Material from columns originally published in September 1971.

Buzz and Hatchet Go Courting

McBride McFadden wants to know whether Dr. W.G. Gamble Jr., of Bay City, Michigan, remembers the time they went courting together. That was in the days before the impressive string of degrees was added to William's name, and he was just plain Buzz Gamble. McBride, who was then a tall, thin chap, had been nicknamed "Hatchet" by Sam John Montgomery, who claimed to see a marked resemblance between a hatchet and McBride's head. That was to pay McBride back for saying Sam John's very square jaws made him look like a tomcat.

When Buzz and Hatchet first began "feeling their oats," they became smitten with two of the prettiest little girls in town—a blonde, and a brunette who was staying at her house. The blonde was Louise Epps and the brunette was Mattie McCollough. The fact that the girls in no way returned the young sports' adoration did nothing to discourage their enthusiasm.

It was then the custom for grown men to wear stiff white collars—the higher, the more stylish. I believe P.S. Courtney, who was himself doing some heavy courting during those years, could wear the highest I ever saw, for his collars were truly works of art in the haberdashery line.

Now, Buzz's father was also a tall, thin man, and his collars were plenty high, too. This Buzz knew, so he secretly borrowed one for his own foray into society. Hatchet slipped one from his father's assortment of the Gates-ajar variety. That was the kind that stood up straight, but the two points were pressed open, hence the name gates-ajar. This was very stunning on someone with an Adam's apple like Hatchet's.

The boys were sure they looked very handsome, notwithstanding their tight, short pants and long, black stockings, held above their knobby knees by inch-wide bands of woven elastic.

Buzz's father, Dr. W.G Gamble Sr. and his wife. Please note Dr. Gamble's high collar. *Photograph courtesy of W.E. Jenkinson III.*

Epps Street as it looked when Buzz and Hatchet went courting. *Photograph courtesy of Williamsburgh Historical Museum.*

The Epps house as it looks today. It remains in the Epps family. *Photograph by Linda Brown.*

The flowing well at Academy and Kelley streets was one of several in Kingstree. *Photograph courtesy of Williamsburgh Historical Museum.*

Pooling their resources, they bought a small box of Lowney's chocolates, and a-courting they went. A long walk through dusty, unpaved streets added nothing to the appearance of their high-topped black shoes, which they had painstakingly greased with Vaseline, but they finally arrived at the home of Mr. and Mrs. D.J. Epps on Live Oak Avenue, where Mr. and Mrs. (Janette Epps) Stanley Inman now live.

But there shyness overtook the boys, and Buzz hid the precious candy under his cap on the hat rack in the hall. Incidentally, no man or boy would have thought of going outdoors without a cap or hat on his head. Soon after Buzz and Hatchet made it into the parlor and were seated opposite the girls of their dreams, they heard Louise's father coming, and the young sports were scared half out of their wits.

Not only was Mr. Epps a big man, he was a big tease. When he entered the door and took one look at what was in his parlor with his little daughter and her guest, there was a long moment of silence, during which the boys in their high collars were sure they plumbed the depths of human misery. Finally, Mr. Epps broke the silence. "Why, Buzz," he remarked most cordially, "I didn't know that was you. At first I thought it was a jackass peeping over a whitewashed fence."

The little girls burst into giggles, but the boys couldn't make a sound. Buzz tried to wriggle, and it was only then he realized nobody had thought to warn him that the chair in which he was sitting had been freshly painted. He was stuck tight. Panic seized him. With a mighty jerk, he got to his feet, bringing the chair with him. Then, with all his strength, he shoved with both hands against it, one foot kicking for dear life.

With a sudden ripping and tearing sound, the chair pulled loose and fell over backwards, but before it hit the floor, Buzz had bolted through the door with Hatchet close on his heels. The male habit of a lifetime prompted the boys to grab their caps—and the candy—as they galloped by the hat rack, leaving Mr. Epps holding his sides with laughter. They didn't stop running 'til they reached the flowing well, which was at the corner of Kelley and Academy Streets. There they stopped to swear off women for life and remained to eat the candy.

Material from columns originally published in March 1952.

Lily

For a short time during the Second World War, we had a jolly little housemaid, about eighteen, whose name was Maria. Though her smooth, healthy skin was so dark it glistened in a bright light, she insisted that everyone call her Lily.

She was crazy about military uniforms, and rank made no difference at all to her. She corresponded by postal cards with many soldiers and sailors, the penciled message on each card vowing eternal love and a promise to be true to him forever. Some days our mailbox was jammed with letters for Lily, who proudly passed them on to me to read. Often the steamy remarks by the girl-starved males, which had set her to giggling, left me speechless, but Lily had to share her mirth with somebody, and I was at hand. Besides, those letters were most unusual documents.

Writing to men in uniform was mostly a game with Lily, but she had a way with men at home, too. Apparently, she had that indefinable "it" made famous by beautiful Clara Bow as the it-girl of an earlier generation. Though Lily wasn't even pretty, she had been born with that mysterious something in a woman's chemistry, which calls to men as surely as clover calls to bees though prettier flowers might be nearby.

One day Lily wrote a soldier at nearby Fort Jackson that she had decided to marry him the following weekend. The next day when I started to the post office, she gave me a single card to mail. Once there, I idly glanced at the penciled address: *To the President of our Country, Washington, D.C.* When I turned the card over, my eyes bugged to read: *Dearest F.D.R., I am going to marry a soldier. Please let the Navy know. Love and kisses. Lily Jones.*

When I could catch my breath again, I dutifully mailed the card, but the joke was too good to keep. I sent it to the *American Legion Magazine*, and when

I received a check for three dollars in payment, I gave it to Lily. She was glad for the money but could never see the point of the joke.

Nor did she marry her soldier after all. When she learned by grapevine telegraph that he had taken off to Europe without letting her know, the things she said about him and his ancestors won't bear repeating, and she mailed a card to "Mr. Hitler, Germany," telling him to catch that so-and-so Buck Private, but he needn't bother to kill him, just put him in jail for life so he couldn't bother any more nice Christian ladies.

It was that same weekend that a tall sailor with a big potbelly and a huge slew-foot hit Kingstree looking for Lily. She had never even heard of him, but he said that he had been the buddy of one of her pencil pals. The sailor had a discharge of sorts and a pocketful of money. Best of all for Lily, he was resplendent in a military uniform, complete with white cap cocked over one eye and gleaming black shoes that made his slewed feet look like camouflaged boats beginning to part company. Lily joyfully took him on, and they had a high old time every night at the most disreputable juke joints within reach.

One morning when Lily sleepily told me she had danced 'til nearly daylight, I was dumb enough to waste my breath by warning her, "You had better watch your step with that sailor. The first thing you know, he will be gone, and you will be left here to raise his child."

As I shook my head and turned away, Lily said kindly, "Don't you worry about me, Miss Bessie. That guy don't know it yet, but I'm going to marry him in a day or two." I mutely wondered how many other men she had already married and how many wives the sailor already had.

True to her word, Lily herded the big guy to the altar before his enthusiasm for her had time to wane. She quit her job, and she and her man strutted their stuff in a big way.

Then came Saturday morning. The potbellied sailor discarded his sporty uniform, including the jaunty white cap and shining black shoes, and he blossomed forth in a light brown suit with orange stripes, a yellow shirt, a snap-brim hat, and tan shoes shining on his slew-feet. Then he proceeded to take Lily to make merry at first one juke joint and then another, where she laughed and danced with gay abandon.

But—late that night, when the ex-sailor was dead to the world, little Lily silently slipped out of the house and caught a fast train to New York.

Material from columns originally published in April 1970.

The Coward Family

Long ago, when Mr. and Mrs. J.W. Coward lived at 302 Kelley Street in Kingstree, Mr. Coward's youngest child by his first wife, Emma McElveen, was a cute little boy named Joe. He had trouble remembering the ages of his five older sisters. It was the delight of the neighborhood boys to ask the age of so-and-so just to hear the little fellow solemnly recite, "Here's the way they come—Oly, Warny, Stelly, Minny, Jessy, Bubba and the little baby." The girls (Juanita died in her teens) are now Mrs. Leola Parnell, Mrs. Estella Cook, Mrs. Minnie Ashur and Mrs. Jessie Gordon. Bubba was Joe himself, and the little baby was Peden Coward, who later had a younger sister named Mary Agnes. When I was a child, Mr. Coward's father, Mr. Adam Coward, lived with them on Kelley Street. The old gentlemen spent hours dozing in a big rocking chair on the front porch of a small grocery he operated for pastime on the adjoining lot, where the large modern home of Mr. and Mrs. (Frances Harper) I.V. Campbell now stands. He was short and stout and had an enormous bushy beard turning gray, but he only chuckled when boys occasionally tried to tease him by calling him "Mr. Santa Claus." I never saw him without his wide felt hat, which bore no resemblance to St. Nick's headgear.

Mr. and Mrs. W.M. Vause lived near the Cowards. Each of their sons, Zeno, Jim, Ed and Joe, was a live wire in his own right, but Jim and Ed were the most active at that time. The Vause girls, Mattie, Mary and Fannie, were gentle in their ways. For some forgotten reason, Mary's nickname was "Reaky."

One day Mr. Adam Coward made a deal with Jim and Ed Vause to paint his name in black letters on the front of his little grocery, which was already painted white. The boys gleefully alerted their schoolmates to watch for their sign. They did a good job on the bold black lettering against the white

The Coward House as it looks today. *Photograph by Linda Brown.*

background, but they left a space between the letter "A" and the rest of the name. Instead of ADAM COWARD, the sign read A DAM COWARD. Most likely the old man enjoyed the joke and would have been satisfied to make Jim and Ed do a repaint job. But their father took a sterner view and there was quite a to-do about the episode.

About the same time, some bold, black lettering mysteriously appeared on a white board fence by an outhouse in the Gilland's back premises, which ran parallel to Kelley Street. It read, "God is Love," but nobody admitted knowledge of its origin, so pretty soon it, too, went the way of the vanishing Indians. But I'll bet there are at least a hundred people in Kingstree today who still remember that sign.

Material from columns originally published on September 24, 1970.